Bakhtin
PRIMER

PETER LANG
New York • Washington, D.C./Baltimore • Bern
Frankfurt am Main • Berlin • Brussels • Vienna • Oxford

Carolyn M. Shields

Bakhtin
PRIMER

PETER LANG
New York • Washington, D.C./Baltimore • Bern
Frankfurt am Main • Berlin • Brussels • Vienna • Oxford

Library of Congress Cataloging-in-Publication Data

Shields, Carolyn M.
Bakhtin primer / Carolyn M. Shields.
Includes bibliographical references and index.
1. Education—Research.
2. Bakhtin, M. M. (Mikhail Mikhailovich), 1895–1975.
I. Title.
LB1028.S46   370.72—dc22   2006037478
ISBN 978-0-8204-8188-3

Bibliographic information published by **Die Deutsche Bibliothek**.
Die Deutsche Bibliothek lists this publication in the "Deutsche
Nationalbibliografie"; detailed bibliographic data is available
on the Internet at http://dnb.ddb.de/.

Cover design by Lisa Barfield

The paper in this book meets the guidelines for permanence and durability
of the Committee on Production Guidelines for Book Longevity
of the Council of Library Resources.

© 2007 Peter Lang Publishing, Inc., New York
29 Broadway, 18th floor, New York, NY 10006
www.peterlang.com

Printed in the United States of America

Table of Contents

1   Living in Time and Space 1

2   Communication in a Pluralistic Society 35

3   Dialogue and Dialogism as a Way of Life 63

4   Living in a Carnivalesque World 97

5   Schooling With a Difference 129

     References 179

     Index 185

Living in Time and Space

Chronotope

Bakhtin borrowed this term from relativity theory to express the inseparability and intersection of space and time

Heteroglossia

the presence of two or more voices or discourses, generally expressing alternative or conflicting perspectives

Dialogue

not just talk, but openness to difference

Carnival

through its spontaneous, free, and familiar interactions, carnival offers a temporary way of experiencing the fullness of life

Too much educational research is tired, trite, and recycled—seldom moving us forward in our ability to successfully reform schools and to passionately engage children and youths in meaningful learning. There is a tendency among researchers and practitioners to seek simplistic answers to questions seen as black or white, to rely heavily on prepackaged prescriptive programs purporting to be "best practice," and to ignore the tensions and complexities of the educational landscape. The work of Mikhail Mikhailovich Bakhtin (1895–1975) has the potential to free us from such impoverished approaches and binary thinking and to challenge us with complex and truly original approaches to teaching, learning, and leading.

Bakhtin's work offers powerful, innovative ideas—**chronotope, dialogue**, **heteroglossia,** and **carnival**—that hold in them the potential for meaningful change. Too often, though, educators nod knowingly when his name is mentioned in connection to these concepts without ever having taken the time

to probe their depths, possibly because Bakhtin's work is difficult. He does not prescribe easy answers. There is no single or universally desirable approach broken down into a number of sequential steps. There are, in fact, more questions and conundrums than ready answers. Even so, his work challenges us and moves us into a deeper understanding of ourselves, the **pluralistic** and often conflicting environments in which we live, and the problems of communication and of comprehension that confront each of us in the complex world of the twenty-first century. It is for that reason that his work has much to offer educators and educational leaders who want to better understand themselves, their professions, their relationships, and their worlds.

pluralistic
describes societies with numerous distinct ethnic, cultural, or religious groups

Praxis
implies putting an idea into practice, often meaning the notion or moral and ethical practice

In recent years, scholars and practitioners of educational leadership have become increasingly concerned about the quality of research and instruction available to guide the thinking and action—the **praxis**—of educational leaders. In this decade, this is apparent in the proliferation of taskforces related to the preparation of educational leaders in many American states, the expansion of models of leadership training, the abundance of new books displayed on publishers' tables at various academic and practitioner-oriented conferences on an annual basis, and the widespread dissemination of a report by Dr. Art Levine (2005). In this report Levine specifically criticizes the American nation's leadership preparation programs as being deeply flawed, suffering from irrelevant curriculum, low standards, weak faculty and little clinical instruction, and doing little more than dishing out higher degrees to teachers in programs that are invariably based on weak scholarship only loosely tied to practice. His arguments are neither new nor totally unfounded; one commonly hears those and other similar complaints repeated as an endless refrain. Innumerable studies and books about educational leadership appear to be simply old ideas repackaged with glossy covers, resulting in a field still fractured by alternative perspectives and lack of consensus.

In part, in reaction to this situation, the early

twenty-first century research scene is dominated by a renewed emphasis by the National Science Foundation on studies that pose significant questions that cannot only be investigated empirically, but which will result in data that are objective, quantifiable, and generalizable. (See for example the six scientific principles identified as underlying "all scientific inquiry, including education research," Shavelson & Towne, 2002). The hope is that scientific research will give us answers; it will show educators a clear path to reforming schools, to creating environments that are "successful"—at least conducive to learning for all children. There is a need to move beyond the current situation and overcome the tendency of educators to, as the title of an article by Cuban (1990) expressed it, engage in "Reforming, again, again, and again."

Another equally serious critique of much educational writing and thinking today is that it is atheoretical with little in-depth understanding of concepts or perspectives that may hold in them the seeds of new ways of thinking, teaching, leading, or learning. Many scholars, writing about educational leadership, for example, are content to make simplistic statements about such giants as Foucault or Bourdieu, to cite from secondary sources, but rarely go beyond a simplistic or unitary reference to delve into the depths and nuances of their work. There are few comprehensive analyses of how the theories might actually relate to or inform new ways of thinking about educational leadership. This book is an attempt to delve deeply into the work of Mikhail Bakhtin and to explore the potential of his ideas for breathing new life into educational praxis.

Bakhtin the Man

On March 7, 1975, arguably one of the modern world's most creative and innovative thinkers died at the age of 80. Since the first translations of his work into English in 1970, Mikhail Mikhailovich Bakhtin, generally known to the West as a Russian literary critic and philosopher of language, has

become progressively more respected for his systematic philosophy and social thinking. It may seem strange that a writer whose major works focus on such difficult authors as Goethe or Rabelais or Dostoevsky could be of increasing interest to educators in North America, but such is the case.

Although still most frequently known and studied by those whose disciplinary interests are literary, many of Bakhtin's major concepts have considerable potential to change the ways in which we think about education and educational leadership (both formal and informal). His approach to the study of the novel went well beyond the semantic and stylistic analyses of other critics. As Bakhtin explored various literary genres and devices, he was engaging in a "lifetime inquiry into profound questions about the entire enterprise of thinking about what human life means" (Booth, 1984, xxiv). As Bakhtin explored the cultures from which great works of literature emerged, his understanding of the central aspects of times and cultures provided novel ways of approaching the world in which we live and in which we engage in education.

Much of Bakhtin's writing has not survived his life and the sometimes tumultuous times in Russia through which he lived (the Bolshevik Revolution, the Stalinist purges, and World War Two). One lost manuscript that might have been of particular import for educators was *The Novel of Education and Its Significance in the History of Realism* (Holquist, 1986, p. xiii). Although the loss of the official copy may have been unavoidable due to the destruction of a publishing house during WWII, the explanation for the loss of Bakhtin's own copy is somewhat more colorful. Perhaps suggestive of the lack of esteem in which he held his own work, the often repeated story is that because of the scarcity and high cost of paper, he had started using pages (from the end) to "make wrappers for his endless chain of cigarettes" (p. xiii).

Subsequent to his completion of a university degree in St. Petersburg in 1918, Bakhtin worked for a while as a school teacher before taking a position

in Leningrad at the Historical Institute. It was while he was a teacher in Nevel, a West Russian city, that the first "Bakhtinian Circle" came together—a group of intellectuals who enjoyed debate and passionate discussion about literary, political, religious, and cultural topics. His first major published work, *Problems of Dostoevsky's Art,* appeared in 1929, with other significant works following periodically thereafter. In Russia, his career was not without interruption and difficulty. In 1923, he was diagnosed with a bone disease that led to the amputation of a leg in 1938. Perhaps because the publication of his work on Dostoevsky came shortly before his exile in Kazakhstan in the same year (likely due to his association with the underground church), his impact was, for a time, muted. Even so, he continued to write. In 1940, he completed and submitted his doctoral dissertation on Rabelais but was prevented from defending it until after the war. His defense caused such an uproar that the academic community was split into two camps, with his examining committee recommending approval, but the wider community winning the day and denying him his doctorate. Only in 1965 was *Rabelais and Folk Culture of the Middle Ages and Renaissance* finally published.

In 1971, on the occasion of his 75th birthday, a "public conference was held on his work and in the published papers of this meeting the claim was made by a distinguished Soviet linguist" (Morris, 1994, p. 2) that writings signed by Voloshinov and Medvedev, about which the authorship is still disputed, had largely been written by Bakhtin. The debate is mostly of academic interest in that the authorship of the works pertaining to education is not disputed; nevertheless, it is one further reminder of the controversial and difficult path of Bakhtin's career. Despite the challenges of his life and controversies surrounding some of his work, he is becoming established in the West as an important sociological and philosophical thinker and in Russia is a "much revered figure, being perceived as a voice that kept faith with traditional values and freedom during the darkest years of Stalinist terror" (Morris, p. 2).

Bakhtin for Educators: What Does He Offer?

In this section I provide an overview of the major concepts to be explored in this primer—concepts that, taken together, constitute a new way of thinking about the role of educators and educational leaders. This is a challenging task in that Bakhtin's ideas are iterative, almost repetitive, and conceptually inseparable. It is impossible to categorize them into neat chapters and topics. One idea runs into the other, circles around, and gains new meaning as it is re-examined in the light of the most recent nuance. For that reason, I am encouraged by the words of Booth who wrote in his introduction to Bakhtin's *Poetics,* "repetitiveness is not repetitiousness" (1984a, p. xxxv). When concepts are first introduced they may seem strange and disconnected; once explored, they take on new meaning; revisited in the light of a previous point, they begin, not only to make sense, but to offer clearer insights and new approaches.

I start with several caveats. I am not here providing a comprehensive treatment of Bakhtin's work. For that, there are many other good sources (see References); here I focus solely on ideas that hold potential for educators who want to better understand how to create schools in which all students from many cultures, backgrounds, and languages, may live and learn together. To accomplish this, I take some concepts explored by Bakhtin in his writing and use them for the stated purpose, without exploring all of his nuances and interconnected pathways. Here I am certain Bakhtin would approve for I find solace in his own words. In speaking about the *chronotope*—the first concept we shall engage, Bakhtin wrote that

> The special meaning it has in relativity theory is not important for our purposes, we are borrowing it for literary criticism almost as a metaphor (almost, but not quite). What counts for us is the fact that it expresses the inseparability of space and time. (1981c, p. 84)

In like fashion, I take his concepts, not as they hold special relevance for literary theory but for educators arguing that what counts for us is the ability to see

more clearly the depths and breadth of our endeavors.

I take more seriously Bakhtin's proposition that the frame is always in the power of the framer, and that there is an outrageous privilege in the power to cite others (Emerson, 1984, p. xxxvii). Bakhtin explained that we should keep in mind that

> the speech of another, once enclosed in a context, is—no matter how accurately transmitted—always subject to certain semantic changes. [Indeed] any sly and ill-disposed polemicist knows very well which dialogizing backdrop he should bring to bear on the accurately quoted words of his opponent, in order to distort their sense (1981d, p. 340).

I in no way knowingly distort Bakhtin's meaning but I am nevertheless conscious of the privilege and power inherent in using his words (and those of others) to build an argument and present a new theoretical perspective of interest to educators.

Overview

With those caveats, I now provide an overview of the topics to be introduced in this book. First I describe and explore the theme of *chronotope,* the inseparability of space-time. As a literary term, space-time is opposed to two other kinds of time. The first is **adventure time** in which all events are controlled only by chance. In this concept of time, there is no **agency,** no possibility of complexity, for nothing can be planned or anticipated. In adventure time, we are simply puppets, never changing, but moving at the whim of others who pull the strings.

The second is *adventure time mixed with everyday life.* In this time concept, in order to show transformation, we are presented with one crisis after another followed by "rebirth" (1981c, p. 115), much as happens to comic book heroes. Here the effects of chance are manipulated to demonstrate the possibility of learning or change—new life following a disaster or catastrophe. In this time, we may change, due to unforeseen, external circumstances, but we have no influence or control over what happens to ourselves or others.

Adventure time
a way of looking at life according to which all events are controlled only by chance.

Agency
the ability to act, to exercise one's power to shape and control one's own life

Public square
refers to the
central square area of a
community, which was often
surrounded by public
buildings in ancient times
and was open to everyone

To avoid these artificial ways of thinking about life, Bakhtin presents the *chronotope*—life as it were in the **public square,** life lived in the full awareness of temporal and spatial realities which provide the "power to expand" and grow. The chronotope, unlike previous concepts, emphasizes the agency of individuals within the realities of space and time. We are not simply puppets, nor are we comic-book characters. We have the ability to take charge of our living and learning.

If, as educators, we began to take seriously the interplays of time and space and to understand the socio-cultural-economic-political and demographic implications of the contexts in which our schools operate, we would be less likely to think and act in decontextualized ways. We would better understand how to effect meaningful educational reform because we would recognize the ways in which the past has shaped (and still shapes) our institutions and, at the same time, acknowledge the need to develop systems of education and learning that are futures oriented. Living with a sense of time and space permits us to "destroy and rebuild the entire false picture of the world." Moreover, "the destruction of the old picture of the world and the positive construction of a new picture are indissolubly interwoven with each other" (1981c, p. 169). Exploring the concept of chronotope will permit us to comprehend how Bakhtin's work can help apply this fundamental concept of time-space to the world of the twenty-first century and the schools in which we educate our young people.

The second major concept of importance to educators, one which will be developed in Chapter 2, is that of *heteroglossia*—the multi-vocal and multi-perspectival approach to life that, according to Bakhtin, is inherent in day-to-day interactions. Rethinking the meanings of speech, the word, the sentence, the *utterance* may help to explain the difficulties we often have in communicating across differences—between and among teachers, students and their families. We will develop insight into the importance of listening, of being *actively responsive*

of being open to otherness. Bakhtin's explanation for why there "can be no such thing as a neutral utterance" helps, in part, to explain why so much miscommunication occurs in organizational life; too often those in authority believe they have communicated clearly, but the listener has had no opportunity to develop the requisite skills for understanding.

Chapter 3 extends this concept of heteroglossia to examine two of Bakhtin's most central concepts: **dialogue** and *dialogism*. For Bakhtin, dialogue is not simply words. It is not speech at all, but **ontology**, a way of life. Dialogism overcomes a closed and fixed monologic approach to life and replaces it with living in openness to difference. He writes,

> A meaning only reveals its depths once it has encountered and come into contact with another, foreign meaning: they engage in a kind of dialogue, which surmounts the closedness and one-sidedness of these particular meanings, these cultures. (1986a, p. 7)

Too often educators want to embrace the concept of dialogue, but argue that talking extensively takes too much time when they must move to action. This type of thinking is contrary to Bakhtin's notion of dialogue. It is not talk, not a strategy for communication, but a way of life. Living dialogically means being open to new concepts, new ideas, new perspectives, and thus to those who may be different from oneself. It is important to note that when one moves dialogically towards another, different idea, one does not automatically embrace it, but "returns" to one's own place, inalterably changed. The elaboration of this concept offers one way of helping educators and educational leaders to deal with the increasingly visible and invisible diversity in their schools and to understand how to overcome some of the roots of disparity and conflict that are often so dominant.

In Chapter 4, we examine the concept for which Bakhtin is perhaps best known: the notion of *carnival*. Taking as a prototype the medieval carnival, Bakhtin sees, in what is a temporary way of experiencing the fullness of life, the possibility of chang-

Dialogue

allows one to remain open to the Other, to difference, and to the possibility of new understandings

Ontology

the branch of metaphysics that deals with the nature of being

Hierarchical structures

implicit configurations of power that determine our "proper" place in the world

ing the normal **hierarchical structures** and inequitable power relationships within an organization. He explains:

> All *distance* between people is suspended and a special carnival category goes into effect—the *free, familiar contact among people*. This is a very important aspect of the carnival attitude. People who are in life separated by impenetrable hierarchical barriers enter into free, familiar contact on the carnival square. (1973, pp. 100–101)

To be sure, carnival, as Bakhtin thinks of it, is a temporary event, but one which holds the potential to change forever, in subtle but real ways, some of the barriers to communication and relationship that exist in institutional life. This chapter focuses on what Bakhtin means by carnival and its implications for educational organizations.

In the final chapter, I put the pieces together and explore ways in which taking seriously the Bakhtinian concepts of chronotope, heteroglossia, dialogue, and carnival can be foundational to new ways of thinking about, living in, and leading, educational organizations. Here the emphasis will be on new ways of thinking and being in the world in which a focus on relationships, on dialogism (rather than monologism), and on outsidedness—another of Bakhtin's important ideas—will permit the educator to embrace the challenging task of educating students in heterogeneous schools to take up their roles in a rich, complex, and diverse society.

Some Textual Explanations

Before proceeding, I need to add some explanatory notes about some of the choices I have made in this primer. In terms of citations and references, where I draw on material from a commentator, a translator, or an editor, I use his or her name, as well as the date and page. Where I cite Bakhtin himself, to avoid repetitiousness and redundancy, I simply indicate the year of the translation I am using and the page reference. Further, because I am concerned here with the concepts, I do not attempt to enter the debate about authorship, nor do I attribute the citations to multiple authors. Where Bakhtin's translators have italicized words or phrases, I remain faithful to their original without further comment; where I choose to italicize for prominence or clarity, I indicate that the emphasis is my own. Sometimes, one finds variations in the spelling or words such as dialog or dialogue; sometimes variants are used as in dialogic or dialogism, carnival or carnivalesque. Again, where I cite, I use the form from the specific editions cited; where I use my own words, I try to remain consistent. At the same time, however, I sometimes cite from various translations of the same work in order to provide the version in which a specific concept seems most clearly articulated. Finally, although I sometimes explicitly extend Bakhtin's thinking to include both male and female pronouns, I cite him as he wrote—a product of the conventions of his time and place, confident that his use of male pronouns will neither detract from the depth and power of his thinking nor prevent twenty-first-century readers from engaging with him. With these caveats and explanations, we now turn to the powerful ideas of Bakhtin himself.

The Chronotope: Time and Space

As previously indicated, the chronotope focuses on how we live in time and space—whether in fixed, passive, closed, "completed" modes that restrict growth and learning, or in the variable, active, open, and always-becoming modes that characterize human existence. Bakhtin defines the chronotope, for his purposes as the "inseparability of space and time (time as the fourth dimension of space!)"; he continues:

> Time, as it were, thickens, takes on flesh, becomes artistically viable; likewise, space becomes charged and responsive to the movements of time, plot, and history. This intersection of the axes and fusion of indicators characterizes the artistic chronotope. (1981c, p. 84)

Talking about some alternative ways of being that are found in literature (remember we are using his literary discussions as our "metaphor" for life at

this point), he suggests that there are three basic ways to live in this world. The metaphor is only partial, as always in Bakhtin's work, in that he also explains that a "real-life chronotope of meeting is constantly present in organizations of social and governmental life" (p. 99).

Overcoming Adventure Time

In the first instance, in earlier times, one focused on life as an adventure. Here, one lived, not in real space and time, but in a heroic mode, controlled only by chance. There is no agency, no personal responsibility, simply the forces of life pressing in on, propelling, and ultimately, "creating" the character. He suggests, for example, that in this mode, a shipwreck only needs a sea, but which sea is immaterial. Space is interchangeable and the wreck could as easily have occurred on a shoal in the Bosporus, the Adriatic, or the Aegean Sea as off the coast of Maine or Florida. In the world of education, we can easily identify educators who live in this world of chance. Practices of schooling that assume children are interchangeable and that one can find and implement one "best practice" without regard to individual differences or contextual specificities are also good examples of this kind of thinking. Educational policies, as well, rarely attend to contextual differences and hence deny the real significance of chronotope.

Teaching today is a challenging task. As schools become more demographically diverse, the forces of history and social mobility play an ever increasing role in the identity-creation and self-concept of students and teachers alike. Educators are not only required to understand and address the diverse needs of children as never before, but they have begun to realize the futility of taking approaches that ignore the specific location of children in their classes. Attempting to creating meaning and enable learning by using decontextualized and generalizable curricular materials is akin to living in adventure time.

No Child Left Behind (NCLB)[1] and other waves of reform have multiplied the challenges of educators in that they have too often been accompanied by unprofessional approaches that deskill the teacher and administrator, encouraging them to narrow the curriculum or to teach to the test as though adventure time were a reality. One challenge, for example, relates to the increasing pluralism of religious and spiritual perspectives represented in our schools. Educators rarely know how to deal with children whose families are Muslim or Buddhist or Hindu. Moreover, because the law says that there must be separation of church and state; the common interpretation is that there can therefore be no talk of spirituality in the building. The educator resorts, once again to living in adventure time—taking no account of the rich and diverse context and oblivious of the need to address political and educational change. Bakhtin explains that "it goes without saying that in this type of time [adventure time], an individual can be nothing other than completely *passive,* completely *unchanging*" (1981c, p. 105).

A second type of person, Bakhtin suggests, lives in part in a world of adventure and in part in the real world. There is no "evolution in the strict sense of the word; what we get, rather is crisis and rebirth" (p. 115). Here the individual moves from crisis to crisis with no consideration of the importance of a specific context and with no understanding of how to respond in meaningful ways. It is not so much that people who live half in adventure time and half in the real world ignore context and the interplay of time and place, they are simply too busy to consider it.

We also know educators like this—educators who make of every day a time of crisis, moving from "fire" to "fire"—always concerned about what the parents or the Board or someone else might think or say, never stopping to really listen to or understand the deep concerns of these stakeholders. For educators living in this bifurcated world of adventure and real life, the glass is always at least half empty. Every challenge, every new policy mandate, every new curriculum reform, every demographic or fiscal change is a crisis, an occasion for resistance, for

despair and, at best, for survival. Educators who live partly in adventure and partly in the real world are reactive. There is little or no consideration of the need to build community, to develop relationships, to enhance awareness, to focus on interactions, or to facilitate learning and growth.

Living in "Biographical" Time

Biographical time
time lived with full knowledge of the context shaped by the intersection of time and space

A third way of living, Bakhtin suggests, is to live fully in the intersection of time and space, in **biographical time,** as it were. Here, life is "constituted by the public square" that site in ancient times which represented the unity of the state and its rules and processes and where the fullness of life was evident to all. Bakhtin writes:

> Here the individual is open on all sides . . . Everything here, down to the last detail, is entirely public. It is fully understandable that under such conditions there could not in principle be any difference between the approach one took to another's life and to one's own. (1981c, 132).

Living in the public square requires the individual to attend to the words, thoughts, and actions of those around him. It is life in recognition of the mutuality of human existence and experience and in reflection about how to improve conditions. This is not to say that the individual does not have a rich, inner life of introspection and dialogue; indeed, it requires that one take time to reflect on both individual and public life.

We are united both by time and space. We come together, unified by both, acknowledging the political and social exigencies as well as the individual. We are united in our common humanity and in our mutual respect and care for one another and thus cannot simply live from crisis to crisis.

In later literary conventions, in which "man's image was distorted by his increasing participation in the mute and invisible spheres of existence," he was "literally drenched in muteness and invisibility" (1981c, p. 135). Moreover, he became "multi-layered, multi-faceted. A core and a shell, an inner and an outer, separated within it" (p. 136). As we shall see in

more depth later in Chapter 3, this fragmented way of living is in contrast to one in which the layers and the facets live in constant tension, in inner dialogue with one another, to create a fully conscious, thinking, responsive, and growing human being.

According to Bakhtin, the key to living in space-time, in the chronotope, is to recognize their inseparability. We cannot understand the present without knowing the history (social, political, cultural, geographic) of a particular place. At the same time, though, history does not *determine* the present. Everything is dynamic; places, societies, cultures, and individuals all evolve in complex ways. Comprehension requires taking this dynamic complexity into account. There is no fully evolved character, no completed human being, one lives in the fullness of time, in "all the contradictory multiplicity of the epoch" (p. 156) in such a way as to portray all of its manifold contradictions. Sidorkin (2002) in talking about this phenomenon argues that a "fully consistent message simply does not capture the complexity of moral life" (p. 156). For Bakhtin, this is not only true in the fullness of the chronotope, but more completely developed in his theories of dialogue and polyphony to be explicated later. One must live fully aware of his or her status as "one who is evolving and developing, a person who learns from life" (1981a, p. 10).

Learning from life is the key. We do not bounce from crisis to crisis never learning about how to take more control of our own lives. We do not live, oblivious to the world around us, conscious only of our own wants and needs. Instead, we live *in* the world—attending to how past forces have made us who and what we are, conscious that we can grow, learn, and change as we continue life's journey.

Centripetal forces

forces that pull us toward a complete and coherent "center" and hence prevent constant reflection and growth

Overcoming Centripetal Forces

Centrifugal forces

seek to keep things apart, unfinished, incomplete, ensuring they are fodder for reflection and change

We live conscious of a struggle between **centripetal forces** and **centrifugal forces.** The former constantly strive to pull us towards a complete and coherent "center" and hence to prevent constant reflection and growth. The latter, centrifugal forces,

seek to keep things apart, unfinished, incomplete, ensuring they are therefore fodder for reflection and change. The educator who understands this tension comprehends that everyone in the school, herself included, is evolving and developing, learning and growing. There is no giving over of education to chance, no throwing up one's hands in a passive display of inactivity, overwhelmed by the changing social conditions and increasing pressures and demands on today's schools. Instead, the educator is sensitive to the plurality of experiences brought together in his or her school community, and to the multiplicity of needs, concerns, challenges, and opportunities they provide. There is no one "best" practice in this educator's lexicon, no one "right" way, but a myriad of approaches used to determine the best ways to teach a particular child in a specific context. When an educator rejects the centripetal forces, she is able to take seriously the lived experiences, beliefs, values, and traditions of individual children in the school as well as the family and community groups from which they come and to find ways to use these varied experiences as a basis for learning and the making of meaning.

These educators are not paralyzed by inertia when they are confronted with statistics about education today. They are not crisis mongers nor are they passive observers. Instead they engage fully with the challenges presented by their educational contexts. For example, in America in 2002, 16% of children—more than 11 million—lived in poor families (families whose income was at or below the federal poverty level of $18,850 for a family of four). Of these, black and Latino children were significantly more likely to live in families with low incomes, with 58% of black children (5.8 million) living in low-income families in 2002 (up 4% from 2001) and 62% of Latino children (7.8 million—up 1% from 2001) (see Douglas-Hall & Koball, 2004). Educators, faced with such statistics do not throw up their hands, blame the society at large, engage in deficit thinking, and reject agency or responsibility; rather they identify ways in which they may help all chil-

dren to achieve similar levels of educational success in terms of access, outputs, and outcomes (Farrell, 1999).

Sometimes the data present significant challenges to educators, themselves often born into the dominant middle-class and thus unable to identify first-hand with many of the experiences of their students. In the United States, of course, the dominant middle class is white and Christian. However, in 2000, according to the U.S. census, 18% of children over the age of five spoke a language other than English (U.S. Census, 2000); 76.5% of homes were Christian, 13.2% reported being non-religious, and 10% of the population identified adherence to another religious tradition (www.adherents, 2005). Further, at the end of the twentieth century, the traditional categories of "minority and majority were inverted in the four states of Hawaii, New Mexico, California, and Texas with nine other states with populations between 36 and 40% 'minority' status" (Majority, 2005)

Educators who live fully in the chronotope of time and space are cognizant of the need for new understandings and new approaches to take account of such statistical realities. Rather than engaging in nostalgic longing for a return to more homogeneous school populations, they find new ways of approaching their work. They may reflect on the theories of Palmer (1998) who urges educators to create spaces in which the differences and paradoxes of diverse communities and multiple perspectives may be included. Or they may promote new ways of thinking about such topics as curriculum and **pedagogy,** building on the definition of Grumet (1995) of curriculum as "the conversation that makes sense of things" (p. 19). Whatever the approach, they take account of the ways in which time and place make their context and their students unique, necessitating novel pedagogical strategies.

Pedagogy
refers to all of the elements involved in the process of educating, including the methods and the underlying principles

Authority and Experimentation

It is important here to note that the chronotope of time and space does not simply require living in the present moment without regard for past or future.

Indeed, it is most important not to conceptualize the past as an "epic" past, "walled off from all subsequent times by an impenetrable boundary, isolated (and this is most important) from that eternal present of children and descendants" (1981a, p. 17). Instead, we must recognize the complex interactions among past, present, and future. Educators must become aware of how the intersection of past, present, and future may result in different learning approaches and characteristics for different groups of children. Those who come from situations of oppression, or expulsion, or children who have faced the realities of war or natural disaster or refugee camps will hold very different assumptions, perceptions, and values which they bring to bear on a given learning situation. The image of a "wall" or "fence" may be quite terrifying to some children whose freedom and mobility have been constrained by such structures; for others, who may have helped their parents build fences to protect their fields and gardens from predators, the same image may be much more reassuring. A tale of a sea journey might similarly conjure for some the perils of escaping a great danger or perhaps even recall the deaths of close family or friends, while for other children it may be associated with the pleasant experiences of a family vacation. There are no authoritative meanings inherent in the words or concepts themselves—something educators must begin to take seriously.

Bakhtin explains that if we consider the past as epic, a glorious rosy time in which, as Voltaire's (1759) *Candide* so often exalted, "everything is for the best in this best of all possible worlds,"[2] then we are confusing "absolute past" with time; we are creating a "valorized hierarchical category," in which the rules and traditions of the past continue unbroken to the present, constraining us, and limiting our ability to respond to new situations. It is this incorrect view of the past, confusing time as the fourth dimension with an incorrect concept of time as "absolute" that prevents change from occurring.

Unless we differentiate between "absolute past" and the time/space continuum in which we live, we mistake and misuse authority. Bakhtin is clear that "in a patriarchal social structure, the ruling class does, in a certain sense, belong to the world of "fathers" and is thus separated from other classes by a distance that is almost epic" (1981a, p. 15). Here is another idea Bakhtin repeats in his writing:

> The authoritative word is therefore located in a distanced zone, organically connected with a past that is felt to be hierarchically higher. It is, so to speak, the word of the fathers. Its authority was already *acknowledged* in the past . . . therefore authoritative discourse permits no play with the context framing it, no play with creative stylizing variants on it. It enters our verbal consciousness as a compact and indivisible mass, one must either totally affirm it, or totally reject it. (1981d, pp. 342–343)

Too often educational leaders uphold existing rules and traditions, oblivious to the power relations implicit in them, oblivious to changing conditions, oblivious to the need for change. We demand that a child speak English (or whatever the language of instruction is) without regard for how such a demand might constitute a subtractive notion of education (Cummins, 1989) and how it might reduce learning to memorizing of concepts rather than offering the opportunity for the creation of meaning. Failing to understand when and why it might be important to permit communication in a home language and when the use of the common language of communication might be appropriate is but one example of such rule-following.

A reified concept of the past is what Bakhtin calls "monochromic and valorized (hierarchical); it lacks any relativity, that is, any gradual, purely temporal progressions that might connect it with the present" (1981a, p. 15). Moreover, thinking of the past as absolute and authoritative isolates it from "personal experience, from any new insights, from any personal initiative in understanding and interpreting, from new points of view and evaluations" (1981a, p. 17).

This explanation of epic time is important. As educators if we hold fast to the "word" of our forefathers, we permit no creativity, no possibility of reform

to enter our consciousness. In part, this helps to explain why educational reform is so difficult. We pay lip-service to the need for reform; we verbally embrace the tenets of the latest innovation; but at the same time, we have not understood how firmly entrenched we are in thinking of the past in epic terms. We fail to permit an understanding of the ways in which past contexts interacted with tradition to create certain solutions and structures and we fail to permit creative variants that might be more relevant to our current contexts. We are locked in what Bourdieu calls our **habitus,** our affirmation of the past as hierarchically higher than the present, and are unable to engage in the "play" required to permit change.

The present, Bakhtin argues, "is something transitory, it is flow, it is an eternal continuation without beginning or end; it is denied an authentic conclusiveness and consequently lacks an essence as well" (1981a, p. 20). For Bakhtin, and for us, this is such an important concept that he reiterates the point repeatedly:

> The present in its so-called "wholeness" (although it is, of course, never whole) is in essence and in principle inconclusive, but its very nature demands continuation, it moves into the future, and the more actively and consciously it moves into the future the more tangible and indispensable its inconclusiveness becomes. Therefore, when the present becomes the center of human orientation in time and in the world, time and world lose their completedness as a whole as well as in each of their parts. The temporal model of the world changes radically; it becomes a world where there is no first word (no ideal word) and the final word has not yet been spoken. (p. 30).

Here, we need to pause to explore what significance this difficult but compelling vision of the present (in its relation to past and future) might hold for educators. As an example, let us consider some current thinking about diversity and multiculturalism in school contexts. Only a few years ago, when many American educators thought about diversity in education, the focus was solely on the desegregation orders following the decisions related to Brown

Habitus

Bourdieu uses this term to represent norms and traditions that define what is possible or normal within a given field vs. the Board of Education. The situation was explained simply. Where there were schools with only (or even primarily) white or African American children, educators were to take measures, most frequently bussing, to ensure a more equal mix of students in each school. More than 50 years after the decision, in the early years of thetwenty-first century, there are indications that these acts have not accomplished the desired effect of equalizing outcomes and opportunities for white and black children in America's schools. Moreover, there are a number of new challenges. "White flight" and housing and real estate policies in many cities have resulted in many schools and neighborhoods being largely segregated once more, with white children in suburbia and blacks in the inner city, but this pattern no longer tells the whole story. The present is neither "whole" nor conclusive and the "facts," explanations and conclusions no longer hold as "absolute truths." There is a "rest of the story," a continuation, in Bakhtin's terms. The bright future envisaged by those who drafted the desegregation orders and the more recent consent decrees that prompted legislation requiring bussing and/or other types of corrective action has not been achieved. There is still inequity among black and white students with regard to the multiple outcomes of schooling. One indication is statistics related to student graduation which show that 7.9 percent of white students, compared to 13.6 percent of black students and 27.5 percent of Hispanic students fail to graduate from high school. Statistics related to student retention, suspension, and discipline show similar patterns of inequality.

As educators wrestle with these facts and try to look in tangible ways toward the future, other pieces of information also come into play to support Bakhtin's rejection of fixed and authoritative understandings. New patterns of immigration have resulted in changing interpretations of citizenship; groups aside from African-Americans are also facing difficulties and need to be included when we think of power inequities and under-representation.

Perhaps because of the controversial nature of

inter-racial relationships (the final U.S. anti-miscegenation law—outlawing inter-racial marriage—was repealed in November, 2000, in Alabama), educators have been silent about the growing numbers of bi-racial, inter-racial, multi-racial or multi-ethnic students in our schools. As we look in the present that continues into the future, we become aware that on the 2000 census, 6.8 million people reported identification with more than one race (Jones, 2005). Multiculturalism in the present and the future, of necessity, looks quite different from that of the epic past. The new faces of schools and classrooms require new understandings, revised curriculum, a more diverse educator workforce, and new pedagogical approaches if we are to develop spaces in which all children feel included and which promote equitable environments for teaching and learning.

Living Self-Consciously and With Introspection

Living in this rapidly changing world in which one responsibility of educators is to prepare students for a future that we do not, indeed cannot, know, requires educators to have a strong sense of their own identity, their own humanity, and what it means to educate students. To have this sense of self, we need to become aware of ourselves as socially located individuals, and as Bakhtin suggests, to examine the degree to which we are sociologically or characterologically typical, our habitus, our spiritual profile, even our very physical appearance (1973, p. 48). All of these aspects, Bakhtin claims, should be the subjects of our introspection and self-consciousness.

This introspection is essential to understand our location in the time-space of our world. When we identify our sociological location, it is not to take an unyielding position, locating ourselves in an ideological, political, or cultural reality; rather, it is so we can better understand those with whom we come in contact, ready to be open to them and their realities, to learn and to become more fully human. It is to recognize the assumptions we hold that might need to be challenged, our knowledge gaps that need

to be filled, and so forth. In the previous quotation, Bakhtin (or at least translator Rostel) used a term most commonly associated with the sociology of Bourdieu—the word "habitus."

For Bourdieu, culture is composed of a variety of fields (such as education, the state, religion, and political parties). (See Swartz, 1997.) Each field occupies positions that have developed over long periods of time and which reflect their possession of various forms of capital. The possession of social, economic, and cultural capital has led to each field's development of its own traditions, rules, and practices. Bourdieu used the term *habitus* as a way of explaining the regularities and norms that have developed in each specific field; for example, in public education in North America, our norms provide for class sizes between 20 and 40 and require children to attend school until age 16. These concepts appear to be firmly entrenched in our educational habitus. Bourdieu explains that

> habitus tends to generate all the "reasonable" and "commonsense" behaviors (and only those) which are possible within the limits of these regularities, and which are likely to be positively sanctioned because they are objectively adjusted to the logic characteristic of the field, whose objective future they anticipate. At the same time . . . it tends to exclude all 'extravagances' ('not for the likes of us'), that is, all the behaviors that would be negatively sanctioned because they are incompatible with the objective conditions. (1990, pp. 55–56)

Bourdieu's implication is that choice is therefore bounded by what we know; Bakhtin, on the other hand, seems to suggest (and clearly does later) that there is a way forward. Here the first step is introspection—carefully examining what it is that we believe and why, how we have come to our positions, what constrains us from thinking in new ways.

A simple example comes to mind related to the issue of scheduling the school year and school day. When confronted with a request to consider implementing a balanced calendar (one that reduces some of the long summer vacation and inserts longer breaks between terms), or to move from a traditional

year-long schedule to a semester approach to secondary schooling, or even, as some have recently, to change from having a morning and an afternoon recess and lunch hour to two "nutrition breaks," most people respond negatively. Forces of tradition come to the fore, making it difficult to be open to new possibilities and new approaches. However, each of these changes, once adopted, has proven to offer new opportunities for teaching and learning for children sometimes disadvantaged by traditional schedules and structures.

On a deeper and more critical level, it is the same sense of finality and our unquestioning acceptance of the past that contributes to the difficulties many minoritized students have in formal education settings. When we ignore issues of class, culture, race, ethnicity, or socioeconomic status and forget that in North America, at least, formal institutions of education were established by white middle-class men to perpetuate the overriding values of a society dominated by these very white middle-class men, we are once again falling into the epic trap. We fail to understand the deep roots of many prejudices, assumptions, and experiences. For example, educators often pathologize the experiences of children who come from situations of poverty, decrying the situation to be sure, but assuming that until the government or another social agency has "fixed" the problem, there is nothing that can be done to ensure equal educational outcomes.

In some ways, this is reminiscent of those who combine the modes of adventure and real life, in that we focus on crises and refuse to assume responsibility or to acknowledge agency. We fail to differentiate between opportunity to learn and ability to learn, making disparaging comments about children who come to school without clean clothes, too hungry to concentrate on their lessons, rarely having had anyone read to them or teach them to use scissors or crayons. We too quickly relegate them to remedial classes, relying on implicit authoritative assumptions from our "fathers" about what a good student looks, acts, talks, and smells like.

Authoritative word

an idea, spoken or implicit, that we feel compelled to obey or act on because of its inherent authority

We adopt **authoritative words** and ideas from the past—rarely stopping to think about their impact on children from non-dominant groups. We wonder, for example, why children from some immigrant groups (often Asians) tend to do well in school while some minority children from our own country (American Indians or African Americans, for example) are typically less successful. At the same time, we reject the explanation of sociologist John Ogbu (1992) who describes secondary and oppositional characteristics among those who have been oppressed or discriminated against; we consider them to be superficial generalizations and point to individual exceptions. We fail to self-consciously reflect on our role in perpetuating epic stories that trap certain groups in "authoritative past discourses," and deny the impact of past events on present performance. Too often, we actually participate in perpetuating the harm, taking an unexamined word from the hierarchically higher "fathers." We continue, for example, to celebrate Columbus Day—the time when Columbus discovered America, with little heed to the voices of those who argue they were here first and did not need to be discovered.

Examples abound of ways in which we prevent more conscious reflection and action by simply adopting the authoritative word from the past. The point is that unless we begin to live with careful introspection and self-consciousness about such issues, we will neither be able to meet the educational needs of children and youth in today's schools nor be able to live as fully human in a pluralistic world that is constantly undergoing change and renewal.

Looking to the Future

We have examined the problems related to the assumption of an epic and authoritative past as well as to an unself-conscious and non-introspective present. But Bakhtin's chronotope is also future oriented. He is clear that the boundaries are always permeable, that the historic past connects to the biographic present and the unspecified future. He suggests that

in our enthusiasm for specification we have ignored questions of the interconnection and interdependence of various areas of culture. We have frequently forgotten that the boundaries of these areas are not absolute, that in various epochs they have been drawn in various ways; and we have not taken into account that the most intense and productive life of culture takes place on the boundaries of its individual areas and not in places where these areas have become enclosed in their own specificity. (1986a, p. 2)

Bakhtin explains that we have failed to engage in a differentiated analysis of areas of culture, especially the "lower, popular ones" which have much to teach us. We ignore the skilled tools of the worker and praise the verbal gymnastics of the academic; we overlook the ways in which young children from less advantaged families have learned to navigate public transit systems, to shop, prepare food, and perform a myriad of domestic skills far beyond the reach of most coddled middle- and upper-class children; we make fun of the rogue, the "fool," the "clown"—and fail to see the wisdom or merit in their alternative approach to life.

At the same time, Bakhtin argues, we categorize and simplify what should not be reduced to simple explanations. Thus, a book like *Uncle Tom's Cabin* may be admired during a time of slavery, but then forgotten once slavery exists no longer. An account of serfdom is likely set aside once serfdom has ended. The experiences of survivors of Native American residential schools may be seen as inconsequential once those schools have been discontinued. However, both the historic significance and future import of these and many other events are lost if they are seen as simply artifacts of a specific past situation. In other words, they still have much to teach us. Speaking now of literary works, Bakhtin states: "Trying to understand and explain a work solely in terms of the conditions of its epoch alone, solely in terms of the conditions of the most immediate time, will never enable us to penetrate into its semantic depths" (1986a, p. 4). He elaborates: one "cannot live in future centuries without having somehow absorbed

past centuries as well" (p. 4). This is not to deny the critical importance of the present, simply to remind us that it cannot be closed off. In fact, "everything," he says, "that belongs only to the present dies along with the present" (p. 4).

Bakhtin says:

> It is precisely the *zone of contact* with an inconclusive present (and consequently with the future) that creates the necessity of this incongruity of a man with himself. There will always remain in him unrealized potential and unrealized demands. The future exists, and this future ineluctable touches upon the individual, has its roots in him. (1981a, p. 37 Italics mine)

Many authors over the years have talked about the importance of a zone. The term appears in science as in a "fault zone," in geopolitical discussions as in "war zone," or, the North Zone of Afghanistan. In classical management theory, Chester Barnard (1886–1961) believed that each person has a "zone of indifference," a range in which he or she would willingly accept orders without consciously questioning authority. His belief was that it was up to the organization to provide sufficient inducements to broaden each employee's zone of indifference so that the manager's orders would be obeyed. The term "zone" is also applied in statistics to identify a range of scores within which any variance is deemed not to be statistically significant. Vygotsky addresses the zone of proximal development—a space in which one can best be taught and learn. Thus he asserts that "learning which is oriented toward developmental levels that have already been reached is ineffective from the view point of the child's overall development. It does not aim for a new stage of the developmental process but rather lags behind this process" (p. 1978).

Zone of contact
refers to Bakhtin's belief that persons need to live in contact and in communication with others

Bakhtin here uses the concept of a **zone of contact** to express one of his most important ideas: the importance of living socially, in contact and in communication with others, learning from interaction at the boundaries, always aware that "the individual is either greater than his fate, or less than his con-

dition as a man" (1981a, p. 37). Bakhtin's zone of contact emphasizes one's orientation towards an "inconclusive present"—one in which there are always "unrealized potential and unrealized demands" (p. 37). The dynamic tensions and inconclusiveness of the present lead, therefore, to an orientation that is both present and future oriented. Nothing one does or says will be the final word. To participate fully in an inescapable future, a person must be aware of a sense of incongruity, of incompleteness. Nothing about this incompleteness suggests one can abrogate one's responsibility to live fully in the present; yet, at the same time, it implies the need to create oneself to face the demands of both present and future.

Creating Ourselves

Bakhtin is clear that creation is not the same as invention. As we create ourselves, we acknowledge that "every creative act is bound by its own special laws, as well as the laws of the material with which it works" (1973, p. 65). For example, a human being cannot fly (as the fated experiment of Daedalus and Icarus has demonstrated) because there are physical laws which we cannot circumvent. However, in our conscious selves, we can learn to live by our "unfinalizeability," by unclosedness and indeterminacy (p. 53). We can continually strive to learn new things and attain new heights. Careful reflection on who one is in relation to movements of time and space permits one to

> find one's own voice and to orient it among other voices, to combine it with some of them and to counterpose it to others, or to separate one's voice from another voice, with which it is inseparably merged. (1973, p. 201)

We create ourselves in communion with and apart from others. Hence the educator must be aware of his or her own voice, the ways in which we are similar to others in the school community, as well as the ways in which we are different. More importantly perhaps, Bakhtin suggests that we must deter mine how to orient, how to position ourselves vis-à-vis other voices representing diverse perspectives. There will be times when the educator must stand with some members of her school community and times when it will be important to separate herself even from those with whom she is generally most aligned. Taking a stand against a school board member who wants the final grade in a sophomore French class raised to permit his daughter to compete for a scholarship may be difficult, but it is one time when the educational leader must be willing to stand apart. Aligning oneself with a group of Muslim parents concerned about a policy requiring their sons to shower in communal showers and their daughters to wear what they consider to be revealing gym garb may not be popular in a community in which Islamic traditions are little understood, but it could be a significant educational act. Changing such long-standing policies may lead to the accusation of being "soft" on minorities, being too concerned about "political correctness," being insouciant of the norms and values of the prominent members of the community—but there are times when, despite the fundamental inseparability of oneself with others from a particular social, ethnic, or religious group, one must take a different path.

Bakhtin suggested that our "spiritual profile" is another area in which we need some self-consciousness: it is another way of "finding one's own voice," of learning what grounds us, what guides us—of identifying on what principles we are willing to take a stand, to what pressures we are vulnerable, and so forth. This concept is consistent with the need to acknowledge that the world consists of "organized coexistence and interaction of spiritual diversity, and not stages of an evolving unified spirit" (1973, p. 25). Spiritual certainty too often becomes a way of being closed to difference, of judging ourselves to be morally superior to another whose beliefs may be different. We create ourselves spiritually by being open to a diverse and complex world.

Bakhtin explains that "the unified, dialectically evolving spirit, understood in Hegelian terms, can

give rise to nothing but a philosophical monologue" (1984a, p. 26). Bakhtin posits that this is contrary to the deeply pluralistic world in which we not only must become aware of our own evolving spiritual profile, but once again, open to that of others. For American educators, post 9/11, steeped in the rhetoric that equates the Islamic world with the axis of evil, this is a particularly important point. Unless educators can find ways to understand and interact with the spirituality of students whose backgrounds and positions are different from their own, it will be difficult to create schools that are inclusive and welcoming of diverse perspectives.

It may seem strange to think of a Russian literary critic, a product of what many see as an antispiritual Russia of the twentieth century, speaking about the spirit, but, recall that Bakhtin was exiled for his involvement in the underground church. Despite his sense that we must not hold to any past tradition, religions included, with mindless and unquestioning certitude, there is evidence throughout his writing of the importance of attending to one's spiritual life. The issue, once again, is to acknowledge the possibility of growth and new information, and to avoid positions that are authoritatively superior. Booth (1984) writes of Bakhtin's worldview:

> Commentators dispute about just *how* large those views are—that is, about the degree to which Bakhtin's unsystematic system is religious or metaphysical. To me, it seems clearly to rest on a vision of the world as essentially a collectivity of subjects who are themselves social in essence, not individuals in any usual sense of the word; . . . his "God-term"—though he does not rely on religious language—is something like "sympathetic understanding" or "comprehensive vision," and his way of talking about it is always in terms of the "multi-voicedness" or "multi-centeredness" of the world as we experience it. (xxi)

Whether one calls it faith, or spirituality, defined by Starratt (2005) as "a way of being present to the most profound realities of one's world" (p. 67), God-term or simply a "comprehensive vision," educators need to pay attention to ways in which they are both sep

arate from and related to the rest of humanity and the broader universe.

An Inconclusive Present

Living in chronotope space/time involves paying close attention to context. It requires that American educators understand, for example, that there are no one size fits all answers, that research directed at finding replicable, generalizable solutions to universal problems is misguided. It requires that we must approach the educative task self-reflectively, understanding our own (temporary) location and the assumptions and authoritative voices that guide us. It requires that we live in the knowledge that we are incomplete, always able to learn, to change, and to grow. It requires us, as educators—indeed as human beings—to be willing to change our minds, to learn from others, to admit that we do not have all the **truths,** all the information, all the answers. It requires us to refrain from assuming that our position is *the* position, that our solution is *the* solution, that our way, is *the* way. We must be open not only to other ways of thinking and acting locally, but it is also important to recall that there are other national, geographic, and political contexts in which our ways are foreign, and which, if we are open to new possibilities, have much to teach us. We must overcome our still strong tendencies to hegemonic thought and action, listen to, and learn from the multiplicity of voices in the world around us.

It is not a sign of weakness to change our mind. It is not an indication of moral failing to move away from a deeply held conviction after encountering another, foreign perspective. It is not necessary to see things as black or white, to always take irrevocable stands, to have every position clearly and irreversibly articulated. Instead, as educators, we must acknowledge with Bakhtin that "reality . . . bears within itself other possibilities" (1981a, p. 37) of which we are still unaware. This is, in fact, the topic of the next chapter in which we examine Bakhtin's concepts of monologism, polyphony, and heteroglossia—with a

Truth
according to Bakhtin suggests valuable ideas that allow for dialogic interactions

focus on what it means to live in, and communicate across, difference.

GLOSSARY

Adventure time—a way of looking at life according to which all events are controlled only by chance. Context is irrelevant. There is no agency or control. In adventure time, there is no possibility of complexity, for nothing can be planned or anticipated. We are simply puppets, never changing, but moving at the whim of others who pull the strings.

Agency—the ability to act, to exercise one's power to shape and control one's own life.

Authoritative word—an idea, spoken or implicit, that we feel compelled to obey or act on because of its inherent authority.

Biographical time—time lived with full knowledge of the context shaped by the intersection of time and space, of the past and present, lived with hope for the future. In biographical time, we can exercise agency, develop new understandings, and learn new ways to live and act in community with others.

Carnival—may involve "fun," but it is much more than fun. It is a way of challenging and changing the inevitable inequities of power and relationship that exist in day-to-day life. Through its spontaneous, free, and familiar interactions, carnival offers a temporary way of experiencing the fullness of life, the possibility of changing the normal hierarchical structures and inequitable power relationships within an organization.

Centrifugal forces—seek to keep things apart, unfinished, incomplete, ensuring they are fodder for reflection and change.

Centripetal forces—forces that pull us toward a complete and coherent "center" and hence prevent constant reflection and growth. When we succumb to them, we are unable to exercise imagination, creativity, or agency.

Chronotope—a term Bakhtin borrowed from relativity theory to express the inseparability and intersection of space and time.

Dialogue—is not simply words or speech. Dialogue is a way of life in which one remains open to the Other, to difference, and to the possibility of new understandings, change, and personal growth.

Habitus—a term used by Bourdieu to represent norms and traditions that have developed over time and that define what is possible or normal within a given field (for example, education, politics, or religion). Habitus describes those reason-

able and acceptable behaviors that are likely to be positively sanctioned in a given society. Thus, by exception, habitus explains the relegation of all other behaviors, ideas, and actions that seem incompatible with accepted norms to the unacceptable.

Heteroglossia—the presence of two or more voices or discourses, generally expressing alternative or conflicting perspectives. For Bakhtin, this is the normal condition of existence. The speaker is not solitary, not unitary, but is embedded in the chronotope of time/space and always brings with him or her a multiplicity of possible meanings, voices, and identities.

Hierarchical structures—implicit configurations that determine our "proper" place in the world, including with whom we may interact as equals, to whom we owe deference, and so forth.

Ontology—the branch of metaphysics that deals with the nature of being. It therefore is an expression of what we believe to be the basic characteristics of reality.

Pedagogy—refers to all of the elements involved in the process of educating, including the methods and the underlying principles.

Pluralistic—describes the condition in which multiple influences are present such as a society in which numerous distinct ethnic, cultural, or religious groups are present and tolerated. Acceptance of pluralism generally implies the belief that such a condition is desirable or socially beneficial.

Praxis—implies putting an idea into practice and often includes the notion of moral and ethical practice.

Public square—refers to the central square area of a community, which, in ancient times, was often surrounded by public buildings. It was open to all, permitting public access to the processes of civic life. The public square or agora, for example in Athens, represented the unity of the state and its rules and processes where the fullness of life was evident to all. It was the heart of political, commercial, administrative, and social activity, the religious and cultural centre, and the seat of justice.

Truth—in Bakhtin's world does not imply the authoritativeness or accuracy of a specific idea or belief; rather it suggests an idea of value, an idea with which one may interact dialogically.

Zone of contact—expresses Bakhtin's belief in the importance of living socially in contact and in communication with others, learning from interaction at the boundaries of what we understand and believe to be acceptable.

NOTES

1   This is the name commonly attached to PL 107–110, the 2001 reauthorization of the Elementary and Secondary Education Act in the United States.

2   "Tout est pour le mieux dans le meilleur des mondes" . . .

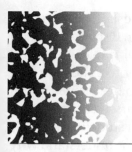

Communication in a Pluralistic Society

Many people who have an excellent command of language feel quite helpless in certain spheres of communication precisely because they do not have a practical command of the generic forms used in the given spheres. Frequently a person who has an excellent command of speech in some areas of cultural communication, who is able to read a scholarly paper or engage in a scholarly discussion, who speaks very well on social questions, is silent or very awkward in social conversation. Here it is not a matter of an impoverished vocabulary or of style, taken abstractly; this is entirely a matter of the inability to command a repertoire of genres of social conversation, the lack of a sufficient supply of those ideas about the whole of the utterance that can help to cast one's speech quickly and naturally . . . (1986b, p. 80)

In this chapter we examine Bakhtin's concept of language and languages, not as scholars of linguistics, but as educators wanting to better understand how to communicate with others, especially those who are different from ourselves. We also approach the topic as individuals for whom the above comment resonates deeply as we recall events in which we were tongue-tied, completely out of our "comfort zone." We may have been baffled by the exclama-

tions of colleagues talking enthusiastically about a new artist and artistic technique on display at the local gallery, or we may have been unable to comprehend the explanation of the computer technician trying to help us to accomplish what to her seemed a simple task. We may have found ourselves face to face with a group of Native American students and their parents, urgently trying to help us understand why the use of "sweetgrass" and a smudging ceremony was not a contravention of the school's drug policy. According to Bakhtin, the possibilities are endless, because of the multi-vocal, multi-perspectival plurality of the world in which we live and work.

In this chapter, we focus on the constituent parts of language or "langue": the word, sentence, and **utterance** as Bakhtin distinguishes them one from another. This provides a basis for thinking about the differences between the monological expression, **polyphony,** and **heteroglossia.** These concepts, as always in Bakhtin's work, do not stand alone; they are both inextricably intertwined with the idea of the chronotope discussed in the previous chapter and with the concept of dialogue which we explore in Chapter 3.

In the next few pages, we examine the ways in which Bakhtin believes the multi-vocal and multi-perspectival approach to life inherent in day-to-day interactions affects our understanding of language and communication. Bakhtin wrote, in his discussion on the *Poetics of Dostoevsky* that

> in a human being there is always something that only he can reveal, in a free act of consciousness and discourse, something that does not submit to an externalizing secondhand definition. (1973, p. 58)

Here, the point is that we are not only never finished; we can never fully know or be fully known. There is always a part of ourselves that only we can reveal, some part of ourselves that we may choose either to conceal or to communicate to others. This acknowledgment that we can never know completely is another warning against generalizations which essentialize others based on a single characteristic

---

Utterance

may be a word, a phrase, or several sentences, but it represents a complete, finished thought

---

Polyphony

refers to a multiplicity of voices that remain distinct, never merge, and are never silenced by a more powerful majority

---

Heteroglossia

the presence of two or more voices or discourses, generally expressing alternative or conflicting perspectives often associated with a specific religious, ethnic, racial, national, or cultural group. The worldwide protests about the publication in February 2006 by a Danish newspaper of cartoons representing the prophet Mohamed are solemn reminders of the dangers of superficial actions and interpretations. Despite the reports of riots and property damage which occurred in some settings, articles that painted all Muslims with the same brush ignored the ways in which many attempted to calm attitudes and spoke out against protests of any kind. A label (such as Muslim) does not, and cannot, tell all about the beliefs, values, or attitudes of the person behind the label.

Frequently when educators begin to discuss how best to communicate, to develop relationships, and trust with one another and their school communities, there is an apparent lack of ability to discriminate between being honest and telling all. Bakhtin here is clear that we have choices. Self-revelation is in part a "free act of consciousness." Once we have come to better know ourselves, as we discussed in the previous chapter, through introspection and a clear sense of how context in its continuum of space/time has shaped us, there is always a part of ourselves that others cannot know unless we choose to reveal it.

A few years ago, with several colleagues, I was involved in a conversation session at a major conference for educational administrators. At that conference, we shared what we called at the time "narratives of identity." In them we talked about our family backgrounds and described some significant incidents that had affected our sense of self. I talked about coming from a white, educated family I could only describe as "privileged," but also shared some of the pain of my divorce. A Muslim colleague, who had left Uganda under Idi Amin's exile and arrived in North America as a refugee, described some painful experiences of discrimination in North America due both to his ethnicity and his family's extreme poverty; classmates who could not know or understand his situation often taunted him for wear-

ing old clothes or not having the sports equipment that would permit him to participate in their games. Another spoke, with humor, about his parents—a white Mother and an African American father who had not been present at his birth and the doctor's initial diagnosis based solely on his "unusual" skin color, of jaundice—jaundice, he indicated, that had never gone away. These stories could not have been known unless we shared them; yet they provided insights into who we were. In fact, several professors, years later, still comment on how our session opened them to the possibility of bringing their personal lives into the classroom instead of keeping them purely separate as they had always been taught to do.

We obviously did not share all the intimate details of our personal lives, but we were willing to be open enough to permit others a glimpse into our own self-consciousness. This last point is important, as I once had a graduate student, a classroom teacher, approach me with some concern. We had been talking about honesty and openness; he was gay, but had never "come out" to his colleagues or students. "Was he being dishonest?" he wanted to know. Being open does not require telling everyone everything, but simply being willing to interact and relate honestly (not completely) with others. Bakhtin wrote:

> In general, the recognition and merging of voices even within the bounds of a single consciousness, cannot . . . be a monologic act; it assumes that the hero's voice will join the chorus. But for this to take place, the fictive voices, which will interrupt and mock a person's true voice, must be subdued and muffled. (1973, p. 211)

At that academic conference, we joined the chorus, and surprisingly, those voices which might have mocked or muffled us in other situations were strangely and silently joined to our own. An examination of Bakhtin's understanding of language will help to explain this phenomenon and demonstrate its central importance to educators.

Speech and Language

Bakhtin rarely defines the terms he uses, despite their newness. He does, however, repeat them in context, over and over, from one work to the next, ensuring we begin to understand his intent. Hence, as I introduce terms in this chapter and explain them, it will become evident that consistent with his characterization of language itself, comprehension occurs as each person, bringing to the text his or her own understanding, creates meaning. At the same time, I attempt to provide an overview and introduction to the terms used here.

In this chapter, key terms include monologic, monoglot, polyphony, **polyglot**, polyphonic, and heteroglossia. It is evident that each makes use of Greek roots such as mono meaning one or poly meaning many. The second syllable of each of these words is, in its etymology, related to the Greek word *logos* meaning *word* or the Greek *glotta,* meaning *tongue.* In their most basic versions, if one can actually have a basic concept in Bakhtin's understanding of linguistics and language, they identify either single or multiple speakers, although, as we shall see, even the concept of speaker is attenuated by Bakhtin. *Webster's New Millennium Dictionary* actually includes heteroglossia, defining it as "the existence of two or more voices within a text, especially conflicting discourses within a linguistic activity as between the narrative voice and the characters in a novel" and indicating that the word was coined by Mikhail Mikhailovich Bakhtin, Russian philosopher. The speaker is not solitary, not unitary, but is embedded in the chronotope of time/space and always brings with him or her a multiplicity of possible meanings, voices, and identities.

In the first few pages of his examination of the work of Dostoevsky, Bakhtin writes:

> A plurality of independent and unmerged voices and consciousnesses, a genuine polyphony of fully valid voices is in fact the chief characteristic of Dostoevsky's novels . . . what unfolds in his works is not a multitude of characters and fates in a single objective world, illuminated by a single autho-

Polyglot
the adjective used by Bakhtin to imply a multiplicity of voices, perspectives, or ways of interacting

rial consciousness; rather a plurality of consciousnesses, with equal rights and each with its own world, combine but are not merged in the unity of the event. (1984a, p. 6).

Polyphony therefore refers to a multiplicity of voices which remain distinct, never merging, never being silenced by a more powerful majority, always interacting in a play or plurality of consciousnesses with one another. The concept of **monologism** or the corresponding adjective **monologic** as used here by Bakhtin therefore is always in opposition to this plurality and hence, by inference, implies a single authoritative voice or perspective, remote, fixed, distant and not involved in the play of human consciousness. Monologism is also used in opposition to the concepts of dialogue and dialogism which will be addressed in the next chapter. The importance of acknowledging multiple perspectives and voices is that

> this mode of thinking opens up aspects of man—above all the thinking human consciousness and the dialogical sphere of man's existence—which cannot be artistically mastered from a monological position. (1973, p. 228)

Just as the author cannot fully develop a character from a single perspective with only a single identifiable trait if the character is to have any depth, so a human being cannot be known, nor can she know herself, without cognition of the multiple perspectives from which she sees herself as well as the multiplicity of lenses through which others see her. Bakhtin explains, "We must renounce our old monological habits in order to become comfortable" in an incomparably more complex world (1973, p 229).

Here his discussion of language becomes a bit technical, but it is important to untangle the threads to better understand not only what he says, but how it can help educators in their daily lives. Bakhtin argues that theories of speech and communication which reduce the communicative act to diagrams depicting the active speaker, the words spoken, and

Monologism
opposite of pluralism, implying a single authoritative voice or perspective that is remote, fixed, and distant

the passive recipient are incorrect and inadequate to describe the communicative act as he sees it. Indeed, he calls such diagrams "scientific fiction" (1986b, p. 68). Bakhtin explains that it is essential to understand and differentiate between the word, the sentence, and what he calls an *utterance*—the *"real unit of speech communication"* (1986b, p. 67). Moreover, in his view, the listener is never passive, but an important and active partner in the communicative act.

Words and sentences are units of language; they are not units of "speech communication" (1986b, p. 73). "We select the type of sentence from the standpoint of the *whole* utterance" (p. 81) because it is the utterance that conveys meaning, that is the unit of communication. We may choose words and sentences to convey meaning but it is only when we have completed a thought, conveyed all that we want to say in that moment about a specific topic, that we have completed an utterance. As Bakhtin conceives of the utterance, it may vary in structure, in length and complexity, but it has clear-cut boundaries. It is not simply a sentence—we have all experienced the discomfort of being "interrupted" in the middle of a thought, when we have only stopped for breath, and then had to request permission to "finish the thought." An utterance is only complete when the speaker cedes the floor, when it is the turn of another to respond, either through silence, words, or action. An utterance therefore is a "link in the chain of speech communication" (1986b, p. 84).

A word in and of itself, Bakhtin says, signifies nothing, although it may also be a complete utterance. In like fashion, a sentence is simply a linguistic and grammatical unit that may or may not contain a complete thought, an utterance. Bakhtin is eloquent on this topic. He writes:

> Words belong to nobody, and in themselves they evaluate nothing. But they can serve any speaker and be used for the most varied and directly contradictory evaluations on the part of speakers. (1986b, p. 85)

A teacher might utter the words "he arrived," to express dismay when a tardy and disruptive student appears at the classroom door. A teenage girl, waiting anxiously for her date to pick her up for the prom, might utter the same words, upon seeing a car pull up at the curb, but this to express excitement and relief. A detective exploring the timing of a particular crime might begin a statement with the same words. In and of themselves, Bakhtin argues the words hold no objective meaning. One must know the context of the utterance, both the physical and emotional contexts, in order to understand the meaning of the words. Bakhtin is self-explanatory:

> The use of words in live speech communication is always individual and contextual in nature. Therefore we can say that any word exists for the speaker in three aspects: as a neutral word, belonging to nobody; as an *other's* word, which belongs to another person and is filled with the echoes of the other's utterance; and finally, as *my* word, for, since I am dealing with it in a particular situation, with a particular speech plan, it is already imbued with my expression. In both of the latter aspects, the word is expressive, but, we repeat, this expression does not inhere in the word itself. It originates at the point of contact between the word and the actual reality, under the conditions of that real situation articulated by the individual utterance. (1986b, p. 88)

If one accepts this argument, it is easy to see why so much of what educators spend time on is ineffective. We sit for hours developing policy, carefully crafting the sentences, "word-smithing" the statements in a strategic plan or statement of values, and then wonder why the words seem empty, why others do not immediately grasp their import and enthusiastically embrace the concepts expressed therein. We send newsletters home, sometimes even having expended the effort to translate them into "foreign" languages, but fail to get the desired result. Too often, no more parents arrive at the parent-teacher interviews after translated invitations are sent home than when communication is purely in English.

Here Bakhtin's explanation connects solidly with that of Lisa Delpit (1988), who comes from a different starting point and a different scholarly position. She states that in every situation there are "rules of power"—rules that benefit those who are already familiar with the context and hence share the power, but that marginalize those who are outside, who do not already understand the context and hence, for whom the words have no meaning. Translating an invitation to parent-teacher meetings, therefore, may still hold little meaning for an immigrant parent who has no formal schooling in her home country. She may wonder what she will have to know, say, or do; what she should wear; how long the meeting will last; whether she should bring food, a younger child, and so forth. Words without context are trapped in the confines of their own specificity without any real means of communicating with others.

There is one more important concept contained in this discussion of words and utterances that must be acknowledged. A word may, in fact, be a complete utterance. A group of teachers, sitting around discussing a specific student's progress, wondering why he seems so verbally bright, when his written work is so sloppy—full of errors and word and letter inversions will pause, smile, and nod their heads, when the school psychologist reports the results of a recent assessment: "dyslexia." Expressed in the context of concern and agonizing effort to help a student succeed, all understand the import of the diagnosis, even though there will be much conversation and exploration needed to achieve any consensus about ways of proceeding to enhance his ability to succeed in the context of formal schooling.

Words in and of themselves mean also little; in fact, they may distort meaning as often as they enhance it, if we are not conscious of the fact that language is always deeply rooted in a context. Moreover, the context is not simply material, but includes emotions, attitudes, and perceptions as well.

Speech and Relationship

Further to the recognition that language is contextual; it is also relational; Bakhtin states that

> when we select words in the process of constructing an utterance, we by no means always take them from the system of language in their neutral, *dictionary* form. We usually take them from *other utterances,* and mainly from utterances that are kindred to ours in genre, that is, in theme, composition, or style. (1986b, p. 87)

I still recall vividly a most painful incident with a friend, who was taking me to a concert. I had shopped carefully for a new dress, proud of its style and colors. When he saw me, he commented on my "garish" dress and failed to understand how the comment had stung. Indeed, he insisted that we look up the meaning of garish in a dictionary, where, to be sure, the first meaning was simply "bright, colorful." The other meanings, though, the ones with which I had grown up (in a different country and context) were there as well: "flashy, gaudy, loud, tawdry, tastelessly showy." The dictionary meanings were of little comfort, despite my friend's protestations to the contrary. Bakhtin offers both insight and help here. He writes:

> When speaking I always take into account the apperceptive background of the addressee's perception of my speech: the extent to which he is familiar with the situation, whether he has special knowledge of the given cultural area of communication, his views and convictions, his prejudices (from my viewpoint), his sympathies and antipathies—because all this will determine his active responsive understanding of my utterance. (1986b, pp. 95–96)

Had both I and my friend recognized that it was not the objective meaning that mattered, but the expressive intent and context of the words in which he was trying to show he had noticed my apparel, I might have more easily overlooked the previous connotations of the word and accepted the "compliment"; in fact, I might have been able to move beyond the "word," perhaps even the "sentence," to understand the depth of affection behind the utterance. Had we then been able to acknowledge the context of close friendship and respect, rather than to focus on the words, the painful exchange might have been more quickly defused and long erased from memory.

It is evident from the foregoing that relationship is essential to understanding, and to the creation of shared meaning (however incomplete). It is for that reason that Bakhtin takes so much care to explain that "language, like the concrete living environment in which the consciousness of the verbal artist lives—is never unitary (1981d, p. 288). Indeed, he identifies two factors that help to determine perception and understanding: who is talked about and what his relation is to the speaker and the degree of their proximity to one another (1984a, p. 170).

This helps to explain why people from a specific group can use language that, when used by another person from outside the group, may be seen as inappropriate and derogatory. It may be permissible for me to complain about the actions of one of my parents or one of my children, but if someone outside the immediate family group dares express the same idea, however gently, I will likely become defensive and reject out of hand the criticism. In like fashion, even heavily value-laden words that are demeaning and prejudicial when used by an outsider, words such as "dyke," "nigger," or "fool" may be said with affection from within a shared relationship. Bakhtin sums up this point, saying, "A particular means of reality can only be understood in connection with the particular means of representing it" (Morris, 1994, p. 179). This is not to say, as Marshall McLuhan once wrote in his famous aphorism, that "the medium is the message," because, as we have seen, it takes more than a medium; it takes relationship in order for understanding to occur.

Bakhtin states:

> To understand another person's utterance means to orient oneself with respect to it, to find the proper place for it in the corresponding context. For each word of the utterance that we are in the

process of understanding, we, as it were, lay down a set of our own answering words. The greater their number and weight, the deeper and more substantial our understanding will be. (cited in Morris, 1994, p. 35)

The closer the relationship, the less likely one will be to take offence when an externally offensive word is used as a term of endearment. The depth of our friendship permitted me and my friend to move beyond the emotional distress caused by our debate over the meaning of "garish" and to maintain our friendship for well over a decade. The more details that have been shared among the teachers about the dyslexic student, the greater and more substantial will be their understanding of his needs, his behaviors, the severity of the condition, and the most appropriate ways of helping him learn. Orienting oneself not only to the words, but to the utterance in its totality—its physical, emotional, ideological context—is one way, perhaps, not to avoid misunderstanding, but to move beyond the confusion to maintain a relationship and develop new meanings.

Another example, more relevant to educators in a North American context at least, comes to mind. One of the most common and widely accepted forms of greeting in our society is the handshake; indeed, books and articles have been written describing the most desirable grasp and frequency. Someone comes into our office and we automatically rise and extend a hand, having been taught that it is always acceptable to do so and that to do otherwise is to appear unfriendly. Some groups, such as the boy scouts or fraternal societies even have secret handshakes. The handshake, though, has not always been so widely accepted. Half a century ago, etiquette books told men to wait for a woman to extend her hand as it was inappropriate for a man to offer the gesture first, perhaps because it might be interpreted as unwanted physical attention; moreover, the woman was taught to simply touch finger tips, not the whole hand.

Even today the handshake is not as universal as we in America would like to believe. In New Zealand, among themselves and their close friends, Maori, for example, press their noses together, intertwining their breaths, in a traditional greeting. Among the Hmong, handshaking is relatively rare, and most women feel uncomfortable shaking hands with an unfamiliar male. Furthermore, because during his lifetime the prophet Mohammed never shook hands with a woman with whom he was not related, there is, in Islam, a religious prohibition against women shaking hands with men outside their family. Numerous stories have been told about non-Muslim educators, reaching out a welcoming hand to a Muslim parent arriving to enroll a student in the school, only to become angry, hurt, or defensive, when the "rude" parent failed to accept the out-stretched hand. We assume that the "other" must adapt to our way of thinking and acting in order for relationship to occur.

This assumption was clearly expressed in an article addressed to Middle Eastern women in America. The author, a multicultural business consultant penned the following advice: "We're dealing with a multicultural environment. If you're a woman from the Middle East, for example, you probably use a very light handshake. But you should use a firm handshake" (Whitmore cited in Harris, n.p.). This utterance fails to acknowledge the importance of context and culture and appears, once again, to assume that all adaptations should come from the non-dominant group.

To return to Bakhtin's point, as the foregoing discussion clearly demonstrates, too much educational wisdom has developed from an **ethnocentric** perspective that fails to consider the context of the word or gesture and that brings us into unnecessary conflict with people whose traditions and values may be different from our own.

Ethnocentric refers to the belief in the superiority of one's own ethnic group

Polyphony and Heteroglossia

For Bakhtin, the notion of centripetal and centrifugal forces discussed in the previous chapter also relates to the ways in which one must understand language. There are, he argues, centripetal forces in

the life of language that are embodied in a "unitary language." This language, though, is frozen, fixed, and unable to become generative of new ideas. For Bakhtin, "a single voice ends nothing and resolves nothing. Two voices is the minimum for life" (1984a, p. 252). Because one is so ineffectual alone—not even alive in Bakhtin's terms—he introduces the concept of polyphony. Polyphony or polyglossia, he states, are "incompatible with the representation of a single idea executed in the ordinary way" (1973, p. 63). Polyphony permits one to become sensitive to the "immense plurality of experiences" (Holquist, 1981, p. xx). It makes us effectual. It is the basic unit of communication in which two people talking to each other begin to come to terms with infinite diversity. "In this actively polyglot world," Bakhtin says, "completely new relationships are established between language and its object" (1981a, p. 12), but also between and among individuals.

Polyphony is the word used by Bakhtin in his earlier writings and seems to focus most clearly on dyads, on individuals in relationship, each learning from the other in the fundamental process of life—the creation of meaning. However, for Bakhtin, the world was more complex, more diverse, richer, and more exciting than could be suggested by two people talking and so he began to use more frequently the term *heteroglossia;* some would say to emphasize the social aspects of communication and human life (see Morris, 1994, p. 113).

Bakhtin posits that "every utterance participates in the unitary language (in its centripetal forces and tendencies) and at the same time partakes in social and historical heteroglossia (the centrifugal, stratifying forces)" (1981d, p. 272). In order for us to participate in social and historical forces, we need to understand how language operates simultaneously at numerous levels (as we saw at the beginning of this chapter). We are well aware, Bakhtin reminds us, of various professional languages—"the language of the lawyer, the doctor, the businessman, the politician, the public education teacher and so forth"

(1981d, p. 289). These languages differ from each other in terms of their specialized vocabularies, but it is important to acknowledge that they are not neutral. As various groups take on certain language for their own purposes, the language becomes stratified, and its "intentional possibilities" are expropriated. Those who use the jargon may be capable of expressing themselves and communicating without mediation, but for outsiders, these languages become *"things,* limited in their meaning and expression"* (p. 289).

When we, as educators, use jargon in talking with people who are not educators, we are using language that we have stratified and expropriated and that prevents others from entering into relation with us. When educators communicate results of standardized tests to the general public using percentile ranks, quartile cut-off scores, NCE levels and so forth, we are leaving ourselves open to misunderstanding and hence, to the unfortunate publication of school rankings and report cards so controversial when they appear in the local newspaper. What the press does in these situations is avoid the use of specialized and stratified language, reducing the gap between test interpretation and parent group, and using language such as "failing" or "passing" that in context may hold different meaning for non-educators. If we do not recognize and appropriately communicate the multi-layered concepts inherent in the notion of a failing or passing school, the contested political and pedagogical ground therein distorts the reality and provides the public with a finalized and frozen understanding rather than allowing for the depths, nuances, and differences of meaning understood by educators.

But it is not only specialized professional language that may lead to barriers of communication and misunderstanding, for all language is vested with multiple, social, and cultural meanings inherent in its use. Bakhtin explains:

> In any given historical moment of verbal-ideological life, each generation at each social level has

> its own language; moreover, every age has as a matter of fact its own language, its own vocabulary, its particular accentual system that, in their turn, vary depending on social level, academic institution . . . and other stratifying factors. (1981d, p. 290)

This phenomenon is not new to parents who sometimes find that the "generation gap" makes it difficult to communicate with their own children nor is it news to educators, often perplexed at how language that meant one thing when they were in school—"gay," "cool," "nerd"—has taken on different connotations and meanings and been replaced by a completely different set of words to communicate similar ideas. Whistling takes on various meanings depending on the culture; the V-for-victory sign should not be used in some countries. Gestures that were once acceptable have become lewd, and so forth. In addition, if this is a difficult problem for children whose families come from ethnic and sociocultural groups similar to those of teachers, it is even more challenging across social and culture groups. At the same time, we err if we believe the problem is confined to a simple semantic one. Bakhtin introduced the concepts of ideology, social situation and class into the above description. These are critically important and he takes pains to elaborate:

> Languages of various epochs and periods of socio-ideological life cohabit with one another. Even languages of the day exist: one could say that today's and yesterday's socio-ideological and political "day" do not, in a certain sense, share the same language, every day represents another socio-ideological semantic "state of affaires," another vocabulary, another accentual system, with its own ways of assigning blame and praise, with its own slogans. (1981d, p. 291)

Anyone who follows national news or world affairs will be able to furnish numerous examples of the fluidity of particular concepts and slogans. "Terrorist" takes on a whole new meaning in the wake of the infamous attack on the New York World Trade Center (9/11); the "Middle East" changes to a less benign "axis of evil"; torture by civilized coun-

tries becomes justified in the name of "national secu-rity;" the Gaza "security" wall is constructed by Israelis but rejected by Palestinians—two historic peoples living side by side in the same land but inter-preting events in diametrically opposed ways. Yet we must be careful not to simplify too much and especially to avoid **essentializing** interpretations or concepts. *Palestinian,* for example, is a term inclu-sive of people with numerous ethnic and religious identities and affiliations.

Bakhtin elaborates:

> Thus at any given moment of its historical existence, language is heteroglot from top to bottom: it rep-resents the co-existence of socio-ideological con-tradictions between the present and the past, between differing epochs of the past, between dif-ferent socio-ideological groups in the present, between tendencies, schools, circles and so forth, all given a bodily form. (1981d, p. 291)

Various perspectives co-exist, contradicting one another, not simply in disembodied ideological debates but in concrete, living, human, embodied form. I am reminded of a comment by a Somali doc-toral student who urged me to be careful to distin-guish between mainstream Islam that focuses on the individual's relationship to Allah/God and an extremist minority group called Radical Muslim that uses Islam as an ideology to achieve its own politi-cal objectives, objectives that are fundamentally contrary, she insisted, to those of the Islamic religion.

Bakhtin takes pains to explain further:

> All languages of heteroglossia, whatever the prin-ciple underlying them and making each unique, are specific points of view on the world, forms for conceptualizing the world in words, specific world views, each characterized by its own objects, mean-ings, and values. As such they may all be juxta-posed to one another, mutually supplement one another, contradict one another and be interre-lated dialogically. As such they encounter one another and co-exist in the consciousness of real people. (1981d, pp. 291–292)

What is particularly important is that we each see through our own eyes, our own upbringing, and

Essentializing

ascribing characteristics to individuals based on their affiliation with a particular group in which a single feature (e.g., skin color) is thought to express essential and intrinsic truths about a person

our own totality of experiences and interactions. We conceptualize the world as we have learned to make sense of it, too often unaware that our view is not *the* view and that others interpret similar situations very differently.

The fact that different people perceive things differently is often graphically illustrated when one seeks witnesses to an accident. A recent news story, for example, carried an account of a computer train that ran into several cars at a level crossing outside of Chicago. The eyewitness testimonies were fascinating in that some reported that their cars had been trapped between crossing arms that had been lowered, while others reported that "the gates were definitely up." The fact that several people recounted such seemingly verifiable empirical facts so differently is surprising. However, it illustrates graphically the importance of perception. If we differ so diametrically about a simple occurrence, how much more might we differ in the ways in which we approach more complicated events because of the complex influences of our cultural, ideological, and class positions!

Consider, for example, how various constituents and groups have interpreted the need to build huge dams (the Glen Canyon or Boulder in North American, or the controversial Three Gorges Dam in China). In every case, the dams were conceived to assist with the flow and control of water, to bring electrical power and economic development to their respective areas. Even so, such feats of human engineering are never universally accepted. Some people's homes and traditional lands are displaced, some historic artifacts may be destroyed or lost forever, and numerous ecological concerns are raised. All of these legitimate perspectives and those whose voices express them are part of the heteroglossia that helps us to understand the world. Of course, there are differences, because, as Bakhtin says, "we envision this 'world at large' through the prism of the concrete social milieu surrounding us. In the majority of cases, we presuppose a certain typical and stabilized *social*

purview toward which the ideological creativity of our own social group and time is oriented" (1994, p. 58).

For some time I have worked with schools on a portion of the Navajo reservation, conducting research, staff development, and evaluations of district policies intended to "narrow the gap" between White, "Anglo" students and Navajo students. Several times I have had occasion to administer surveys and conduct interviews with teachers and parents related to their views on "culture"—asking whether Navajo culture should be taught explicitly or perhaps even required for graduation and/or whether bilingual programs were successfully increasing the achievement of Navajo students and reducing the underlying racism identified by some as a persistent district problem. Inevitably there were differences in responses between the Anglos and the Navajo as well as within each group. Some Navajo parents, wanting their children to experience school success and go on to fulfilling and financially comfortable careers argued for English-only instruction, believing this was the best way to help their children. Most Navajo parents, however, supported explicit instruction in Navajo language and culture and made statements like, "It is very important to know your true identity and to know your own culture." Some expressed the opinion that, perhaps because some parents and grandparents have "lost" some of their culture and hence children do not always learn it at home, that this is a way of helping to preserve it for future generations. Although some Anglo parents were supportive of explicit instruction in Navajo language and culture, others made comments like:

"We live in a society of English."

"We are an English speaking school and nation."

"This is America. We speak English."

"English is the language of the United States and English is an international language!"

"Indian peoples in this area live in America and should be required to learn English."

(And my personal favorite): "Our language is English and we teach that. It is their choice to come to this country to live and be educated." (Shields, 2002)

It is informative to examine these comments through the lens of Bakhtin's explanations. These respondents are seeing through the prism of their immediate social milieu. From this perspective, America is an "English" country and all others who choose to come here should learn English. The social location of many white parents within an English-speaking community made it difficult, if not impossible, for them to recall that the American Indians did not, in fact, "choose to come here" but were here first, and hence, perhaps should be able to make counter-claims for the pre-eminence of Native languages.

Here I am not trying to take either a political or a pedagogical position, (although I am cognizant that my words, thoughts, and choice of illustrations and examples are embedded in my wider political and ideological frameworks); I am trying to illustrate the difficulties of communicating with those whose social locations and historical constructions are different from our own and therefore, to emphasize how essential it is to be able to interact with them. This awareness raises the critically important question (to be examined in some detail in Chapter 5) of how educators, confronted with such conflicting perspectives, might create school communities and implement instructional programs that have any hope of accomplishing either the desired goals or the political mandates of the current system.

Bakhtin adds another comment that serves both as a caution and an explanatory note as we consider this question. He writes,

Any motivation of one's behavior . . . is an act of gauging oneself against some social norm, social evaluation—is, so to speak, the socialization of

oneself and one's behavior. In becoming aware of myself, I attempt to look at myself, as it were, through the eyes of another person, another representative of my social group, my class. Thus, *self-consciousness,* in the final analysis, always leads us to *class-consciousness.* (1994, p. 45)

As we test ourselves, examine ourselves against an invisible but socially acceptable norm, we tend to measure ourselves, our success, our positions against those with whom we share social location. Our self-consciousness is deeply embedded in consciousness of our own class and social location—whether we are aware of it or not. It behooves us, therefore, to become aware that

oppositions between individuals are only surface upheavals of the untamed elements in social heteroglossia, surface manifestations of those elements that play on such individual oppositions, make them contradictory, saturate their consciousness and discourses with a more fundamental speech diversity. (1981d, p. 326)

As educators, we sometimes believe that a board member or parent who opposes us is "out to get us," or wants to destroy everything we have worked for just because there has been a past disagreement or there seems to be a personality conflict. Bakhtin suggests another, more fruitful, way of thinking about conflict. We need to plumb its depths to get to the "untamed elements in social heteroglossia." If we look more deeply at the reasons why some Navajo parents reject having their children learn to speak Navajo in favor of learning English, we may discover a continuing legacy of historical realities: the horrors of the Navajo "long walk," the political designation of certain areas as "reservation" lands, the impact of the official policies that suppressed heritage languages of aboriginal people, policies and practices surrounding Indian boarding schools—all of which infuse current thinking and attitudes towards the dominant "mainstream" culture and suggest to them that maintenance of Navajo language and culture may be inherently "risky."

In similar fashion, a liberal and progressive edu-

cator, wanting to overcome traditional hegemonic practices that marginalize members of minority groups, particularly students of color, may be amazed when confronted with a group of angry students decrying affirmative action policies within the school. Current examples might include Christian students opposed to the inclusion of events such as Ramadan or Hanukkah and the concomitant minimizing of Christian holidays such as Christmas; straight students opposing gay and lesbian student associations or support groups; or white students asking, in the face of cultural groups established for Latino/Latina, Native Indian, or Muslim students, where their cultural group is.

Such perspectives must be taken seriously by educators wanting to promote understanding and create inclusive school communities—schools in which all students feel there is a place for them, regardless of class, ethnicity, language, religion, sexual orientation, or other too often defining characteristics. To do this, educators must understand heteroglossia— the infinite variety of legitimate perspectives that must co-exist and interact on a daily basis within their organization. Moreover, as we shall see further in the next chapter, it is incumbent on educators to develop deep and meaningful approaches to dialogue, and to find ways to model, encourage, and facilitate dialogic understandings. Bakhtin is clear about the importance of this concept; so he writes, "only polyglossia fully frees consciousness from the tyranny of its own language and its own myth of language" (1981b, p. 61).

The Importance of Listening

From the foregoing, it has likely become clear that communication, through spoken words or actions, is a two-way street. It is not enough to speak thoughtfully and carefully, even to painstakingly craft a complete utterance that contains the fullness of your thinking. Making an effort to find the exact word to convey your precise meaning may not effect the desired outcome, because, as we have seen, "the use of words in live speech communication is always individual and contextual in nature" (1986b, p. 88). Moreover, the words themselves, even when they are embedded in the whole intentions and emotional context of the speaker's intentions, are only part of the process. The listener is an active, engaged, and essential presence whose responses shape the meanings inherent in the interaction.

> The fact is that when the listener perceives and understands the meaning . . . , he simultaneously takes an active, responsive attitude toward it. He either agrees or disagrees with it (completely or partially), augments it, applies it, prepares for its execution, and so on . . . (1986b, p. 68)

The listener is so important that who he or she is, what the speaker knows the listener has previously said about a topic, or what both have previously discussed, all shape the ways in which the communication occurs: listeners "also determine our emphasis on certain elements, repetition, our selection of harsher (or, conversely, milder) expressions, a contentious (or conversely, conciliatory) tone, and so forth" (1986b, pp. 91–92).

As an educator, we may have previously had an emotional meeting with a parent who has broken into tears in our office, and we may have responded with impatience or by explaining the rules and regulations. Unless we have found a way to listen deeply, we may have responded to the superficial immediate situation, unaware that the parent is concerned, not only about her son's reportedly aggressive behavior at school, but also burdened by the knowledge of her husband's physical violence at home, his loss of a job, the critical financial situation of the family about to lose its home, and is aware that all of these factors contribute to her son's performance at school. If we have taken the time to listen, we will not respond as though the home factors are inconsequential. Instead, we are more likely to take a concerned, caring, conciliatory tone, using cautious rather than severe language about sanctions and repercussions and will be more likely to try to take

a holistic approach to addressing the family's problems than simply to deal with what had originally
seemed like a simple disciplinary incident. The stance
of the listener, her response, and her situation have
ultimately changed our speech and our interactions.

It is not, therefore, an understatement for Bakhtin
to say that,

> to some extent, primacy belongs to the response,
> as the activating principle; it creates the ground
> for understanding, it prepares the ground for an
> active and engaged understanding. Understanding
> comes to fruition only in the response. (1981d, p.
> 282)

An essential insight from Bakhtin's approach to language is that the listener holds considerable power
to shape the form, the content, and the response to
any situation. Thus, a concerned educator might
well begin to ask oneself, "Why do I talk so much
and listen so little?"

Too often interaction in educational institutions
is monologic. In P/K-12 schools, we teach as though
covering the curriculum by talking about it will help
students to prepare for the test, but Bakhtin's insights
clearly suggest that giving the learner (the listener)
a more active role and taking into account his or
her specific sociocultural location will produce a
more meaningful interaction. We seek a teacher-
proof curriculum, concerned that no extraneous
material interfere with the ability of the learner to
receive the curriculum as a fixed, pre-packaged
whole—failing to put into practice our knowledge
that one must respond to material, make it one's
own in order for learning or growth to occur. In
higher education, we hold classes in large lecture
theatres so that experts in given areas may communicate their knowledge to passive learners—again
forgetting (or at least ignoring) that each learner
makes of the lecture what he or she wants depending on the words actually heard and those lost because
an utterance gave rise to related musings that prevented the next key idea from being heard or understood. We hold staff or department meetings in

which information is tossed off with little opportunity for response or we hold news conferences at which we announce a key policy initiative or research finding, and despite the fact there was no question period, no time for dialogue, and little time for reflection, we are amazed and often angry when our important words have been distorted.

A key lesson here is that we must begin to understand and take seriously the primacy of the listener. To do that, we must speak less.

A Loophole

There are several important lessons to be taken by educators from this brief overview of Bakhtin's concept of language. One dominant message from this whole discussion of language, words, sentences, utterances, and the polyphonic and heteroglossic world around us, is that if we are to succeed as educators in creating the conditions under which all children may be successful, we will speak less and listen and respond more. In doing so, we will begin to recognize that we can never change another person but only the ways in which we understand and present ourselves.

Bakhtin has reminded us that language is not neutral and hence that our choice of words, no matter how careful we are, may result in misunderstandings and hurt if we do not pay attention to the cultural, social, and historic meanings embedded in them. Just making a statement does not imply understanding. Utterances are not objective, but laden with values and emotions, hence the need for care in choosing words. This is not only an additional argument for listening more (although it may supplement the previous point); it is a reminder that we cannot simply make a statement and then leave a situation, believing that because we think we have found an answer, the solution has been either clearly communicated or accepted by those to whom we spoke.

Finally, Bakhtin has developed an argument for the primacy of relationships in order for us to under-

stand our rich and complex world. Two people, he has stated (i.e., relationships in which we can learn and grow) are essential for life. Our world is polyphonic, filled with heteroglossia. There are multiple perspectives, a plurality of consciousness, he says, with equal rights (1984a, p. 6), and we must learn to live fully in this complex world. Note, however, that Bakhtin does not fall into any kind of evaluative comment here. He does not say all perspectives are equally good, equally correct, or equally desirable. He says they have equal rights—rights to be heard, to enter the chorus, to be understood.

Thankfully, he offers what he calls a "loophole." This is not a "way out" in the common sense of the word. He does not say that if we don't like what we are hearing, we can stop listening. He does not say that if we don't like gays or lesbians, Asians or African Americans, Christians or Muslims, lawyers or doctors (substitute any terms you wish), we have the right to dismiss them. He does not say that if we listen long enough or talk loudly enough, we will convince others of our position. What he does offer as a loophole is a way to change the way we have presented ourselves and to offer to another a different way of seeing us:

> A loophole is the retention for oneself of the possibility to alter the final, ultimate sense of one's word. If the word leaves this loophole open, then that fact must inevitably be reflected in its structure. This possible other sense, i.e., the open loophole, accompanies the word like a shadow . . . In condemning himself he wants and demands that the other person refute his self-definition, but he leaves himself with a loophole for the eventuality that the other person will indeed suddenly agree with him, with his self-definition . . . The loophole creates a special kind of fictive final word about oneself; its tone is unclosed and it peers importunately into the other person's eyes, demanding a sincere refutation. (1973, pp. 195–196)

What Bakhtin offers is the possibility to recognize that the self we have created is at least in part fictional. We do not have to remain in the box of the opinions, attitudes, and ideologies that we have cre

ated for ourselves. We can learn, in the light of the other's gaze, to re-create ourselves, to change, and to grow. Moreover, once we have convinced someone else to agree with us, we must then acknowledge the possibility that we will still grow, change, and perhaps even reverse our position. Fixed, final communication does not exist in Bakhtin's worldview.

We cannot change others, but we can change ourselves. We can change how we see ourselves, how we present ourselves to others as caring, flexible, understanding, and open to the possibilities of renewal. This is in fact the hope Bakhtin offers as we move from the basic understandings of life as chronotopic and polyphonic as presented in these first two chapters to a new kind of **ontology** to be explored in the next chapter, a lifestyle in which dialogue is both the means and end of our existence.

Ontology
the branch of metaphysics that deals with the nature of being

GLOSSARY

Essentializing—ascribing characteristics to a person based on his or her affiliation with a particular group in which a single feature (e.g., skin color) is thought to express essential and intrinsic truths about a person. For example, one might hear essentializing phrases such as, "all Chinese students are good at math" or "all African-American students are athletic."

Ethnocentric—refers to a belief in the superiority of one's own ethnic group.

Heteroglossia—the presence of two or more voices or discourses, generally expressing alternative or conflicting perspectives. For Bakhtin, this is the normal condition of existence. The speaker is not solitary, not unitary, but is embedded in the chronotope of time/space and always brings with him or her multiple possible meanings, voices, and identities. (See chapter 1).

Monologism or monologic—always in opposition to pluralism, and hence, by inference, imply a single authoritative voice or perspective, which is remote, fixed, distant, and not involved in the play of human consciousness. These words are also used in opposition to the concepts of dialogue.

Ontology—the branch of metaphysics that deals with the nature of being. It therefore is an expression of what we believe to be the basic characteristics of reality. (See chapter 1).

Polyglot—the adjective used by Bakhtin to imply a multiplicity of voices, perspectives, or ways of interacting.

Polyphony—refers to a multiplicity of voices that remain distinct, never merge, and are never silenced by a more powerful majority, always interacting in a play or plurality of consciousnesses with one another.

Utterance—for Bakhtin the "real unit of speech communication." It may be a word, a phrase, or several sentences, but it represents a complete, finished thought. Once an utterance has been expressed, one is ready to cede the floor to another's response.

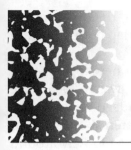

Dialogue and Dialogism as a Way of Life

In the first chapter, I presented an overview of Bakhtin's life and his notion of chronotope to express the interrelationships between time and place and among the past, the present, and the future. In Chapter 2, the focus was on his concept of language: the primacy of the utterance, the nature of the world as essentially pluralistic and inherently heteroglossic. One problem with trying to organize Bakhtin's thinking in the inherently linear fashion required by any text, but particularly perhaps, a primer, is that his work does not break neatly into clear-cut categories. As indicated at the outset, there is much circling around, and there are many reprises and re-iterations of his ideas as we proceed; however, I have divided the chapters in the following way. Chapters 1 and 2 describe the *conditions* under which we live and work, and this chapter and the next offer ways of *acting*, of living life to the fullest in those material conditions of heteroglossia and chronotope. Hence, the focus in this chapter is **dialogue** and dialogism, with the concept of carnival being left

Dialogue

allows one to remain open to the Other, to difference, and to the possibility of new understandings

for the next chapter. Once again, the divisions are not neat, and there is much overlap both backward and forward in this chapter.

Dialogue is, of course, not a new topic. Many (including myself, see Shields & Edwards, 2005) have written extensively about it. Indeed, *dialogue* has been used so frequently and written about so often that the word is ubiquitous, tossed loosely around with almost as many connotations as speakers. In an attempt to both clarify dialogue in the Bakhtinian sense, and to critique and elaborate his concepts where appropriate, I will draw in this chapter, not only on Bakhtin's own work, but on the work of others, especially Sidorkin's (1999) book, *Beyond Discourse: Education, the Self, and Dialogue,* which is an extremely valuable examination of Bakhtin's concept of dialogue.

First it is important to note that, for Bakhtin, dialogue is not simply words or talk (we have seen how meaningless he believed words alone to be); dialogue, though, is ontological—a way of life. It expresses a fundamental orientation to the other, a desire to understand and be understood in relation to an "Other." Some (see, for example, Sidorkin, 2002, p. 92) would argue that in modern times the roots of relational ontology can be traced to Martin Buber who stated unequivocally, "all actual life is encounter" (1970, p. 62) and "in the beginning is the relation" (p. 69). Buber believed that "the basic word can only be spoken with one's whole being: whoever commits himself may not hold back part of himself" (p. 60). Thus, although Buber did not talk of dialogue itself as the basis for **relationship,** he did emphasize the embodied nature of words. Like Bakhtin, Buber acknowledged that we misinterpret the power of words if we believe them to be more than components of language: "basic words do not state something that might exist outside them; by being spoken they establish a mode of existence" (p. 53)— one which for him was fundamentally relational.

Dialogue is therefore the basis of relationship. It is fundamental to a way of life that is changeable rather than fixed, that is open and tentative rather

Relationship

refers to how people interact with and treat one another

than authoritative. Because there are so many casual uses of the word *dialogue,* it is helpful to start with a reminder about what it is not. It is not just talk. It is not, as Bakhtin (or Buber) conceptualize it, only words. It is not simply a way of communicating with other people. Dialogue, as Senge (1990, pp. 240–241) so aptly says, has little in common with *discussion* whose roots are similar to those of *percussion* or *concussion.*

Dialogue is not a semantic device for explaining, convincing, or manipulating others. Indeed, some of Bakhtin's critics (Morris, 1994, p. 9). who seem to overlook the relational rather than semantic basis for dialogue are concerned that he does not adequately recognize the potential for dialogue to be manipulative or hurtful If conceptualized only as words, as verbal exchange between one or more others, outside of oneself, dialogue can be hurtful; it can be manipulative. For Bakhtin, though, dialogue is something greater and, at the same time, more basic. It is a way of life. Dialogue is both the source of meaningful life and an orientation that permeates one's external responses to others as well as one's self-consciousness; it is inherent in both the written and spoken word, in inner and outer consciousness, and in action. As usual, Bakhtin does not offer a neat definition of dialogue, although his explanations recur in almost every extant piece of writing. Simply put, as a starting point, it is appropriate to say that for Bakhtin dialogue is ontological—a way of living life in openness to others who are different from oneself, of relating to people and ideas that remain separate and distinct from our own. Taken together, our actuality and other equally valid and distinct realities therefore comprise a more complete "truth" than can be known otherwise. It is important to note that when we use the word *truth,* we are not discussing the accuracy of the ideas or beliefs one holds, nor are we suggesting a relativistic world, often implied in the common expression, "Who am I to decide?" This is in no way what Bakhtin argues. What he does suggest, however, is the need for all

ideas and positions to be on the table in order for deep dialogue and understanding to occur and for truth to be determined.

I take as the starting point for this chapter, Bakhtin's explication about how text relates to dialogue. I then examine what it means to live in **dialogic relations,** the relationship of dialogue to "truth," the role of **inner dialogue** as key to a moral life, and the importance and possibility of "action" within heteroglossia.

Dialogic relation

a way of relating to one another in the fullness of each person's existence and in the fullness of differences among people

Speech Genres and the Problem of Text

Inner dialogue

occurs when we allow different voices to help us examine our positions

In this section I examine the notion of dialogue in relation to text before turning, in subsequent sections, to examine dialogue and dialogic relations that may occur between and among human beings. The issue of "text" can be problematic. In its origins, text relates both to the late Latin word textus, meaning a written account, and to the older Latin verb texere, to weave or fabricate. Most recently this latter root has led to the revival of the concept of text as structure, as any fabricated "cultural product, regarded as an object of critical analysis" (American English Dictionary online). Hence, text does not always refer to written language but also to cultural artifacts. It is instructive here to read both meanings into Bakhtin's discussion of texts.

Texts, Bakhtin explains, may be both monologic and polyphonic—depending in part on how they are approached by the reader. Thus, if one takes a purely linguistic approach, there can be no dialogic relations. A linguistic approach may focus on the words and individual meanings, but there is no context, and hence no relationship. For a text to be polyphonic, one must enter into a relationship with the words and the ideas. Bakhtin explains that dialogic relationships are "extra-linguistic phenomena." He goes on to say that they

> must not however be separated from the province of the word, i.e., from language as concrete, integral phenomenon. Language is alive only in the dialogical intercourse of those who make use of it. (1973, p. 151)

It is only as we make use of the words to inform us, challenge us, prompt us to debate the ideas, or even to create new ones, that we can enter into a dialogic relationship with a text. Dialogue is related to the word, to speech and meaning, but is not limited to the word either as spoken or written. Dialogue can only exist in the context of relationship. Bakhtin states:

> A scientific article, in which various authors' utterances on a given question are quoted, some to be refuted and others, on the contrary, to be corroborated and supplemented, is an example of a dialogic relationship among directly significant words within the bounds of a single context. The relations of agreement-disagreement, corroboration-supplementation, question-answer, etc. are purely dialogical relationships, although not of course, between words, sentences, or other elements of a single utterance, but rather between whole utterances. (1973, p. 156)

The utterances that are included in the text do not constitute a unified whole, despite an author's best attempt to develop a logical and coherent argument. Once the utterances are expressed, they form the basis for the kind of debate about alternative perspectives that is the basis for dialogic relationships. Thus, one can approach a text ready to engage with it, to examine it carefully, identifying areas of disagreement, of debate, of new questions as well as of corroboration and new insights. A few pages later, Bakhtin compares the tendency to desire a definitive word in a scientific text with man's search for certainty in life:

> The scientific consciousness of contemporary man has learned to orient itself in the complex circumstances of the "probability of the universe;" no "uncertainties" are capable of confusing this scientific consciousness for it knows how to calculate and account for them. It has long grown accustomed to the Einsteinian world with its multitudinous systems of measurement etc. But in the realm of *artistic* cognition people continue now and then to demand the crudest, most primitive certainty [. . .] which cannot possibly be true. We must renounce our old monological habits. (p. 229)

Modernism generally implies the existence of a single true meaning. Hence, over time, we have become socialized, through understandings of science, social and political institutions, and daily life, to believe there is always one best approach, one "best practice," and so forth. We are taught to try to understand what an author *means,* or to discover the truth of the facts as explicated in a text. However, as Bakhtin argues above, even as we approach scientific texts, it is more productive to do so in a spirit of dialogue than from a desire to seek a definitive answer.

For educators, "best practice" has become a mantra associated with almost every new (or newly repackaged) approach or program, even despite considerable conflicting evidence. The notion of approaching text dialogically is an important caution for educators who are bombarded by claims, often in the form of advertisements from textbook companies and producers of curricular materials, that their materials are nationally and internationally recognized, scientifically based, and highly researched, and promising to outperform traditional methods of instruction for all children. We read and believe the text without entering into dialogue with it. We seek simplistic answers because we have been taught to do so. We have not been taught to live with uncertainty, with paradox, and with ambiguity and so we continue to seek packaged solutions to address every pedagogical need. We engage in reform initiatives that have little impact, despite the proliferation of studies that demonstrate the ineffectiveness of doing so. Fullan (1999) argued that "the jury must be in now that rationally constructed reform strategies do not work" (p. 3). Despite our proclivities to engage in more of the same, as educators, we need something different—an entirely new approach. Bakhtin's understanding of dialogue and dialogic relationships may provide the way forward. It certainly encourages us to read with a dialogic and questioning attitude, and with a certain healthy skepticism.

Living Dialogically

In Chapter 2, I introduced Bakhtin's concept of heteroglossia—a multivocal and multiperspectival universe that can only be experienced in its fullness when we live in the midst of it. Bakhtin says of the "languages of heteroglossia" that they are like "mirrors that face each other, each reflecting in its own way a piece, a tiny corner of the world" (1981d, p. 414). They do not fuse or compete for prominence, but like a mosaic, each makes an essential contribution to the total picture.

> They force us to guess at and grasp for a world behind their mutually reflecting aspects that is broader, more multi-leveled, containing more and varied horizons than would be available to a single language or mirror. (pp. 414–415)

The concept is reminiscent of the image presented in a poem by Alexander Pope in 1711 when he talked about climbing a mountain, expecting to see the valleys below, only to find that "Hills peep o'er hills, and Alps on Alps arise" (1951). The image of horizon is also prominent in Gadamer's (2002) concept of understanding as a back and forth, to and fro, endless play of significations. In *Truth and Method,* he states, "understanding is always the fusion of these horizons supposedly existing by themselves" (p. 306). For Gadamer, the emphasis is that our understanding, although limited, is never fixed, but there are times when individual "horizons are present to each other in some degree, where participants see the other's horizon within or perhaps beyond their own" (Shields & Edwards, 2005, p. 81). Moreover, Gadamer writes, "working out appropriate projections, anticipatory in nature, to be confirmed 'by the things' themselves, is the constant task of understanding" (2002, p. 267).

In contrast to Gadamer's concept of dialogue in which horizons tend to merge even if full fusion is impossible, Bakhtin's horizons never merge; "conceptual horizons [. . .] come to interact with one another" (1981d, p. 282). Unlike Gadamer's sense that confirmation may be achieved by things them-

selves, for Bakhtin there are no such fixed meanings or confirmations. Everything is relationship and a specific conceptual horizon simply "introduces totally new elements into the discourse" (p. 282).

Bakhtin states:

> There is neither a first nor a last word and there are no limits to the dialogic context (it extends into the boundless past and the boundless future). Even *past* meanings, that is, those born in the dialogue of past centuries, can never be stable (finalized, ended once and for all)—they will always change (be renewed) in the process of subsequent, future development of the dialogue. At any moment in the development of the dialogue there are immense, boundless masses of forgotten contextual meanings, but at certain moments of the dialogue's subsequent development along the way they are recalled and invigorated in renewed form (in a new context). (1986e, p. 170)

As suggested by our discussion of the chronotope in Chapter 1, time is fluid; its meanings are always subject to reinterpretation, to new meanings as we bring to bear new perspectives, new interpretations, knowledge previously unavailable, and insights as yet unstated. Nothing is finalized; no meanings are fixed; and so our world is a great kaleidoscope of time and space in which we live out our humanity.

When we reflect on scientific understandings of the brain over time, we have an excellent example of Bakhtin's point. There was a time when the brain was considered the seat of all emotions. The ancient Greek physician Galen believed that "epilepsy resulted from stagnation of the cold humors (phlegm and black bile) within the ventricles or cavities of the brain" (Restak, 1984, p. 30). By the late eighteenth century, neuroscientist Franz Josef Gall became convinced that by examining the protuberances on a skull, one could identify individuals with specific talents or disabilities (p. 25). In the late1800s, Morton and Broca, who were both widely respected researchers, conducted craniometric studies, in which they measured and weighed human skulls. They posited, based on what are now known to have been erroneous measurements of skull size, the superiority of the

white man over African Americans or American Indians—with the outcome, Gould asserts, in his 1981 revision of *The Mismeasure of Man,* of three centuries of racism (p. 91). More recently, whole curricula have been designed around such concepts as multiple intelligences (Gardner, 1983) or brain-based learning (see Caine & Caine, 1994; Jensen, 1995)— although I always wonder what kind of learning is not brain-based. The point is, of course, that we keep revisiting and revising the ways in which we interpret almost everything, including the brain, in the light of new science, new revelations, or more subtly, new perspectives introduced into our limited horizons. Even past meanings are revisited, challenged, revised, and introduced in different ways into present theories.

Dialogue, though, does more than simply bring into existence new meanings based on reinterpretations of the past. It is through dialogue that ideas are born. For Bakhtin, as we have seen:

> everything . . . gravitates toward the dialog, toward dialogical opposition, as the center point. Everything else is the means, the dialogue is the end. One voice alone concludes nothing and decides nothing. Two voices is the minimum for life, the minimum for existence. (1973, p. 213)

Dialogue—interaction between at least two people— is the basis of life. There can be no meaningful human existence without dialogue (whether with oneself or others). Dialogue is not the means to something else; it is the end—the goal. This is where Bakhtin differs from so many thinkers who write about dialogue. Burbules, for example, in an important book related to dialogue and pedagogy, is always conscious of the ends of his concept of dialogue. Thus when he defines dialogue, he limits "the term to a particular kind of pedagogical communicative relation: a conversational interaction directed intentionally toward teaching and learning" (1993, p. x). He elaborates, "Dialogue represents a continuous, developmental communicative interchange through which we stand to gain a fuller apprehension of the

world, ourselves, and one another" (p. 8). Although this fuller appreciation may well be one end of dialogue in the Bakhtinian sense as well, it is not the goal. For Bakhtin, dialogue is simply the relation of an individual to the pluralistic world in which he or she lives.

Garrison, writing about dialogue, asserts that

> Most of the discourse on dialogues across differences assumes our primary relation to "Others" is a knowing relation . . . Actually our relations to "Others" are more often aesthetic, ethical, embodied, affective, or even erotic. (2004, p. 94)

Each of these ways of relating to others is a part of what Bakhtin would call relating dialogically. This is consistent with the way in which Buber understands relation when he says, "the relation to the You is unmediated. Nothing conceptual intervenes between I and You" (1970, p. 62). Whatever the aesthetic attraction, whatever the physical association, or the emotional (even erotic) connections, they are direct. We relate to one another in the fullness of our existence and in the fullness of our differences.

There is nothing outside this dialogic relationship. When we accept this fundamental concept, we are in a position to understand the ways in which we learn and grow, the ways in which new ideas take root, form, develop, and become possibilities for action. Bakhtin explains:

> An idea does not live in one person's isolated individual consciousness—if it remains there it degenerates and dies. An idea begins to live, i. e., to take shape, to develop, to find and renew its verbal expression, and to give birth to new ideas only when it enters into genuine dialogical relationships with other, *foreign,* ideas. Human thought becomes genuine thought, i. e., an idea, only under the conditions of a living contact with another foreign thought, embodied in the voice of another person, that is, in the consciousness of another person as expressed in his word. (1973, p. 71)

In other words, relationship—dialogic relationship—is essential for genuine thought. Relationship is, of course, not real if, in Buber's terms,

it is focused on I-it rather than I-thou understandings. Bakhtin voices the same opinion:

> The consciousness of other people cannot be perceived, analyzed, defined as objects or as things—one can only *relate to them dialogically.* To think about them means to *talk with them; otherwise they immediately turn to us their objectivized side.* . . . (1984a, p. 68)

Buber says that people are "wretched" if they "address the ideas with a concept or a slogan as if that were a name!" (1970, p. 65). When we fail to look beneath the name or the label, we cannot engage in dialogic relationships and we are, therefore, both pitiful and wretched.

When we permit prejudice to close us to the human being in front of us, seeing only an American Indian, an African American, a dyslexic child, an ESL learner, a queer student—we cannot enter into a dialogic relationship and we are the poorer for it. Moreover, the interaction must be continual. It is not enough to suspend disbelief, to put aside our assumptions and prejudices for one time only, we must live in constant openness to one another.

The experiences of one of my doctoral students constantly remind me of the dangers of labels. Although Amita has fair skin and blue eyes, her Indian father was born in Lahore; Lahore is of course, now in Pakistan, but before partition when Amita's father was born, it was in India. When Amita went looking for a traditional lehnga cholis (a heavily embroidered fitted blouse and flared skirt) to wear for her wedding, she was accompanied by her parents and an Indian aunt and uncle. Nevertheless, the sales clerk took one look at her and asked why in the world she would want such an item. Amita was labeled based on her skin and eye color and in that instance all possibility of relationship evaporated. (Bakhtin might argue that even this experience was not final, and that there are ongoing opportunities for those involved in the labeling and rejection of Amita as a "legitimate" Indian, to revisit their assumptions and learn from the experience—a re-examina-

tion that ultimately did occur.) At first, Amita's explanations and protestations, urging the saleswoman to look at her father, were to no avail, perhaps because as Bakhtin explains,

> With *explanation* there is only one consciousness, one subject; with *comprehension* there are two consciousnesses and two subjects. There can be no dialogic relationship with an object, and therefore explanation has no dialogic aspects (except formal, rhetorical ones). Understanding is always dialogic to some degree. (1986c, p. 111).

Despite Amita's protests, urging, and explanation, she was an object—a white girl wanting to buy a lehnga; there was no relationship; she was not conceived outside of the stereotype that the woman had set for herself as Amita walked into the store. At some point during the interaction, the saleswoman reconsidered. She interacted not only with Amita, but with her parents, and enthusiastically began helping her to try on the heavy and richly embroidered skirts, carefully adjusting them, pinning them up, exclaiming about how beautiful Amita would be on her wedding day.

Bakhtin says that

> everything lives on the very border of its opposite. Love lives on the very border of hate, which it knows and understands, and hate lives on the border of love, and also understands it . . . Faith lives on the very border of atheism, sees its reflection in atheism and understands it, and atheism lives on the border of faith and understands it. . . . (1973, p. 148)

We begin to understand when we come into contact with opposites—with things we do not understand. When the saleswoman encountered an apparently white, blue eyed Indian woman, she had to confront her assumptions and stereotypes.

This illustration raises the issue of cultural difference and cultural stereotypes. Bakhtin reminds us that "the unity of a particular **culture** is an *open* unity" (1986a, p. 6). Culture itself is fluid, in flux. It changes depending on its location in both historical and biological time. Hence, for example, Amita's father, a

Culture
expresses the customary beliefs, social norms, values, and material traits of a particular group of people

Hindu, was born in India, but in today's world, a person born in Lahore would be Pakistani and most likely a Muslim. Bakhtin continues,

> In the realm of culture, outsidedness is a most powerful factor in understanding. It is only in the eyes of *another* culture that foreign culture reveals itself fully and profoundly . . . A meaning only reveals its depths once it has encountered and come into contact with another, foreign meaning; they engage in a kind of dialogue, which surmounts the closedness and one-sidedness of these particular meanings, these cultures. (p. 7)

I am a Canadian. One day, when an American friend was visiting, and the Canadian national radio station (CBC) was playing in the background, my friend started to laugh. The commentator had talked about Canada being a "kinder, gentler nation." My friend has teased me mercilessly. Over the years, whenever there has been a news story that remotely contradicted the self-conscious image of Canadians as kind and gentle, he has sent me an email message, phoned me at all hours, or mailed me an article, never letting me forget that we characterize ourselves as kind and gentle. His "attack" was especially relentless during the infamous trial of Paul Bernardo and his wife Karla Homolka, for the rape and murder of Karla's sister and two other girls, and the subsequent release of Homolka after serving only 12 years (due to a plea bargain agreement) for complicity in murder with her former husband. The construction of kinder and gentler as seen from outside sometimes appears ludicrous.

So amazed I was at the words of the CBC announcer and his construction of Canadian culture as kind and gentle, that I subsequently, on several occasions, when teaching about culture, recounted the story to my graduate classes in educational leadership. On each occasion, the response was the same: silent stares. It was as though, never having viewed the Canadian context from outside, my well educated and thoughtful students still could not fathom that anything might be wrong with the characterization.

The opposite was also true. A Canadian doctoral student (who happens to be an Ismaili Muslim) and I had often traveled together from Canada to the U.S. to attend conferences and engage in staff development activities on the Navajo reservation. On one occasion, I had to go ahead to attend some pre-conference business meetings in Cincinnati and my friend was turned back at the Canada-U.S. border. I recounted the story at several conference sessions. He had been asked to provide evidence he was presenting at a conference, so he showed the immigration agent copies of the paper we were to present; he was asked to provide evidence he planned to return to Canada: he pulled out the letter signed by his employer indicating he had a job, a wife, and a son, and was an outstanding employee in good standing. He was asked about his TN Visa and informed the official that it was for use when he worked as a staff developer on the Navajo reservation, but that this time, he was receiving no remuneration, only presenting at an academic conference. He was denied entry. Although there are always (as Bakhtin points out) alternative interpretations, in this case we came to believe, based on the questions and our previous positive experiences when traveling together, that the rejection was based on the color of his skin and his foreign sounding name. When I recounted the tale to my academic colleagues explaining why we were not able to present the scheduled paper, they expressed sadness and asked me to convey their condolences to Satish, but none interpreted the incident as related to racial profiling or racial prejudice. The self-conscious construction of themselves as educated Americans from a civilized, tolerant, democratic society prevented them from considering that possibility.

In the previous instances, it took a "foreigner," from a position of outsidedness, to begin to reveal the depths of meaning in the situation to the culture from within which the incident took place. The dialogue was enjoined and, as Bakhtin indicated, participants in both situations began to confront and

to surmount the one-sidedness of the particular meanings.

One further illustration will help to make the point. Some years ago, I invited my oldest son (then in his early twenties and a self-confessed hater of homosexuals) to join me hiking with some friends. I hesitated, and then "warned" him that the men with whom we were going to stay were partners. After some protests and with trepidation, he agreed to accompany me, dreading the encounter but anxious to explore the countryside I so loved. His idea about "gays" had been confined to his own consciousness; he had never met a homosexual man; but he had been conditioned to dislike them by both the media and his father's constant negative outbursts. The first evening, after a day of hiking, exploration, discovery, lots of laughter, good food, and stimulating conversation, he closed the door to my room and said quietly, "Mom, this is going to sound really silly, but Wayne and Chad are really nice!" I had not set out to convince him about how nice my friends were or to eliminate his prejudices. There had been no goal other than the dialogic relationship of spending time together. The different lifestyle of Wayne and Chad was incidental, but as my son encountered them, a new idea began to take shape: "gay men could be nice." As my son's thought came into contact with another, *foreign,* thought, a new consciousness took shape and came into being as he expressed his new insight to me.

I am not suggesting that all dialogical interactions result in such a dramatic turnaround or that this is necessarily the goal of living dialogically, but it does open the possibilities of change and new ways of interacting with others who are different from us. Moreover, the moment of expression was certainly not the end of my son's experience; as we interacted together over several more days and on a number of subsequent occasions, his openness grew—not only to Wayne and Chad but to their friends and to others whom he saw as different from himself.

What my son discovered was a new "truth"—not

an objective, once and for all sort of objective truth, but truth nonetheless. Living dialogically opens us to a very different understanding of "truth" than the one we may have learned as children and it is to this topic we now turn.

Dialogism and Truth

"Truth" is a strange word to use in the twenty-first century—a time when we often think of ourselves as postmodern, as beyond the kinds of fixed truths taught to us as children—truths about mythical characters like Santa Claus, the Easter Bunny and the tooth fairy, or more meaningful and significant truths about the dominance of white people and the need for segregation between Blacks and Whites, or truths about the **exclusivity** of Christianity as the only way to heaven, or whatever we might have believed at one time and then begun to question. Truth, though, is a word frequently used by Bakhtin, albeit with a specific meaning.

Exclusivity
implies that other perspectives, approaches, and beliefs are not valid and that the privilege claimed is the prerogative of one group

Bakhtin writes

> It is essential to emphasize once again that the issue is precisely the testing of an *idea,* of a *truth,* and not the testing of a particular human character, whether an individual or a social type. The testing of a wise man is that of his philosophical position in the world, not a test of any features of his character independent of that position. (1973, pp. 114–115)

First, it is important to note that Bakhtin uses the phrase "a truth." He is not talking about fixed, irrevocable universal Truth with a capital "T."[1] He is talking about the testing of an idea to show something of value, something new as one interacts dialogically with it. For my son, it was his understanding of "homosexual" that was tested and overturned. The experience was not, fundamentally, an evaluation or assessment of my son, his moral fiber, his tolerance, or his wisdom. It was simply an experience of otherness that permitted him to test and modify his own understanding of the world. Bakhtin's words ring true:

The truth is not born and does not reside in the head of an individual person; it is born of the dialogical intercourse *between people* in the collective search for truth. (1973, p. 90)

Had my son not been willing to go hiking with me, he might never have had the opportunity to engage in "dialogical intercourse" and hence to find a new truth about homosexuals.

Note once again, dialogue and **dialogic interactions** are not synonyms for talking, just as it was not the product of a conversation that "convinced" my son to change his mind. It is the totality of the experience in which one human being comes into contact with another (or others) different from himself or herself. Truth as Bakhtin understands it is collective. It can never reside in the heart or mind of a single person, because there are too many ideas, too many experiences, too many cultures, too many artifacts for any one person to have been able to grasp the totality of human existence. No one has traveled everywhere, read everything, met everyone; hence, there can be no truth that resides in an individual apart from the polyphony and heteroglossia that makes up human existence. In fact, Bakhtin says explicitly that "the concept of polyphony is incompatible with the representation of a single idea executed in the ordinary way" (1973, p. 63).

Truth is a word used by other writers both contemporary and classical, but there are almost as many meanings as there are authors. Plato believed, for example, that "dialogue was the rational path to knowledge and the highest form of teaching, and for him these two claims were inseparable" (Burbules, 1993, p. 4). However, it was Plato's particular version of Truth, Goodness, and Beauty as unchanging ideals that led him to this particular teleological view of dialogue as having a definite and predetermined end. Parker Palmer, a contemporary writer, defines truth in a more fluid way, more consistent with the non-teleological conception of Bakhtin. Palmer says that "to teach is to create a space in which the community of truth is practiced (1998, p.

Dialogic interaction

an individual's contact with others with the implication that the individual is open to learning from that experience

90) and then defines truth as *"an eternal conversation about things that matter, conducted with passion and discipline"* (p. 104). He explains that unlike the objectivist, he does not "understand truth to be lodged in the conclusions we reach about objects of knowledge" (p. 104). How could it be, he asked, reminiscent of Bakhtin's words, "since the conclusions keep changing?" Palmer expands:

> I understand truth as the passionate and disciplined process of inquiry and dialogue about itself, as the dynamic conversation of a community that keeps testing old conclusions and coming into new ones. (p. 5)

Palmer believes that "when we reject that with which we cannot become intimate, our lives are diminished" (p. 91) and asserts that in "the community of truth, as in real life, there are no pristine objects of knowledge and no ultimate authorities" (p. 101). "Truth, far from being linear and hierarchical, is circular, interactive, and dynamic" (p. 103). For Palmer too, truth is partial, fluid, a process rather than an event fixed in time; there is an overtone here of at least a temporary resting point that seems more settled and more permanent than what we find in Bakhtin. Yet, for Palmer as well, truth is communal and resides in the community's temporary understanding rather than in an individual consciousness.

Sidorkin, one of today's most insightful explicators of Bakhtin, takes the concept a little farther: "according to Bakhtin truth is not the result of a dialogue, truth is dialogue" (2002, p. 98). It is not the idea or the position to which one comes; it is the process of living open to our heteroglossic world that constitutes truth. Truth is "a number of simultaneous and inconsistent messages rather than one unified message" (p. 157). Moreover, "truth reveals when one can hear and comprehend both or all voices simultaneously" (Sidorkin, 1999, p. 30). Truth is the ability to hear and to hold in a dynamic tension numerous, varied, sometimes conflicting, sometimes intersecting ideas, without having them merge, without trying to reconcile them into a unified

whole. "Truth" Sidorkin argues with Bakhtin, depends on a "multiplicity of different voices for its very existence" (1999, p. 63). Later (2002), he picks up the same idea:

> Polyphony does not imply 'the truth is somewhere in the middle.' . . . The very point of plurality for Bakhtin is constant touching, shifting, penetrating, mutual inclusion of voice. His idea is that multiple voices never merge, never come to a grand ending of a grand narrative, does not in any way mean that the voices do not change each other. Quite the contrary, the interaction is the truest moment of their being. (p. 170)

For the educator, this is an unsettling concept. We are so steeped in processes requiring students to master *the* content, to choose *the one right* answer, to learn a specific method, and so forth, that if we were to take this notion of truth as constantly shifting and polyphonic, it would revolutionize the ways in which we teach and test.

Again, we may find Amita's experiences educative. On one occasion, in a class talking about globalization, in which there was a pervasive "political correctness" about the evils of globalization, the topic of sweat shops and child labor in the Third World was raised. After several others made comments decrying the practice, Amita carefully suggested that there might be another perspective. Some Indian adults, she proffered, believe that, although child labor may be inherently wrong, the answer is not simply to outlaw it or to boycott all materials made in Indian shops. Some poor families find it acceptable to permit each child, in rotation, to spend one year working in a factory in order to keep a roof over the family's heads and food in their mouths; moreover this employment might well permit the other children in the family to remain in school. Taking this approach, Amita explained, might cause each child's education to be retarded by two years, as he or she takes a turn working, but ultimately the whole family would be both more stable and better educated. Amita's class was horrified. How could she support child labor?

The point is not whether or not child labor is inherently wrong. It is not whether we should engage in a boycott of stores that sell products from developing countries produced with generally poorly paid labor. It is not whether or not there are some universal values. The point is that, for the most part, in Amita's class, there was no room for her voice. Her classmates (and unfortunately the instructor) had made up their minds. There was a "right" and a "wrong" and the position was monological, unassailable. In turn, the monologic position prevented the group from grappling with an alternative perspective that might have contributed to their understanding of the global economy. If, in our classrooms, there is no room for dialogue, no place for varied perspectives brought about because of a personal experience, or simply an alternative reading of a situation, we are not only closing down dialogue, we are denying people the opportunity to engage dialogically, to live in the fullness and richness of differences of perspective and opinion.

Truth, understood in this dialogic way, has a fundamentally moral meaning. This is not the same as scientific truth about objects, but emerges from a willingness to hear different words being spoken about the same object. Truth is not in the object but in the dialogue: hence,

> a person of integrity is deeply committed to truth, and truth is being born between us. This requires a commitment to dialogue, a commitment to ascertain the other (Thou art, therefore I am), to discover the human dimension of this world. Thus, the truth is different depending on with whom you are speaking. (Sidorkin, 1999, p. 63)

In the next section, we explore in more detail, the idea that truth may have a moral, yet simultaneously fluid and indeterminate meaning.

A Dialogic Moral Life

It is not only the educator who may have difficulty with Bakhtin's concept of dialogism as indeterminate meaning. Each of us, if we are honest, may

first wrestle with some of the complex ideas, and then perhaps, breathe a sigh of relief when we acknowledge that just as there can be no unity in Bakhtin's heteroglossic world, so there can be no fixed and finalized internal consciousness; indeed doubt is acceptable and normal. It becomes important to recognize that dialogue, as we have conceptualized it to this point, is not only external. We do not only interact with texts or with people, we interact as well with ourselves in an ongoing internal dialogue.

What does it mean to engage in this inner dialogue? How does it relate to living a moral life? Bakhtin says that "nothing changes at all if, instead of outward speech, we are dealing with inner speech. Inner speech, too, assumes a listener and is oriented in its construction towards the listener" (Morris, 1994, p. 42). He continues:

> A dialogic approach to oneself breaks down the outer shell of the self's image, that shell which exists for other people, determining the external assessment of a person (in the eyes of others) and dimming the purity of self-consciousness. (1984a, p. 120)

First, a dialogic approach to ourselves will make it possible for us to relate to others as real people, not simply as labels or symbols. If I take a dialogic approach to myself, I recognize there is much more that I do not know than what I know. I acknowledge that I can undoubtedly learn as much from my students and from those who are my research collaborators as they can learn from me. That knowledge releases me from the pressure of needing to maintain an image, of needing to be "the expert" and so permits me to participate dialogically in the passionate and disciplined inquiry before us.

I recall vividly my uneasiness when, as a young English teacher, I was asked to teach Steinbeck's (1937) novel, *Of Mice and Men*. The novel, as most will recall, not only contains language that some find offensive, but it culminates in one friend killing another. Having been taught never to swear and, of

course, that killing was wrong, I wrestled with the validity of teaching such a novel to my tenth grade class. The internal dialogue intensified when I received calls from several parents asking why I was teaching such an "obscene" book. However, as I heard myself telling them that the language was appropriate for the characters and that the book was fundamentally about friendship between people who were different, not only was I convinced of the book's merits, they gave their consent. When, at the end of the term, one young man told me it was the first book he had ever read from cover to cover, I realized the importance of challenging my own understandings of "appropriate" and "inappropriate" and of finding materials that could reach different students in various ways.

I still struggled with the concept of inner dialogue. I had been brought up in a relatively conservative, Christian home to believe that many things were black and white, right or wrong—things that I now look back on with incredulity and sometimes amusement. I learned, for example, never to use credit but to buy with cash, to always let a man open a door for a woman, that drinking alcohol of any kind was wrong, that those who did well on tests at school were smarter than those who did not, and that, although desegregation was desirable in the abstract, there was no provision in God's plan for inter-racial marriages—all beliefs I refute today. I now look with concern but hopefully more understanding and tolerance on others, like my engineer father, who still tends to see the world in absolutes. It helps me to comprehend his firm faith, to the very last day of my mother's battle with cancer, that the doctors could find the problem and "fix" it.

You can likely imagine some of the struggles I went through challenging my truths, wondering if there was something wrong with me when, as an adult, nothing seemed as black or white as I had been taught. As I read Sidorkin's (1999) own journey and his struggle with the need for certainty, I felt a sense of relief. I was not alone. He wrote: "The self integrates around the need to remain open and unfinished, and around the purpose of dialogue with others" (p. 65). What a strange statement for someone who had learned to believe that the authentic and moral self took a stand and held to it in a never wavering fashion. Is it possible to be both moral and uncertain? Bakhtin certainly argues for that position.

> The single and unified consciousness is by no means an inevitable consequence of the concept of a unified truth. It is quite possible to imagine and postulate a unified truth that requires a plurality of consciousnesses, one that cannot in principle be fitted into the bounds of a single consciousness, one that is, so to speak, by its very nature *full of event potential* and is born at a point of contact among various consciousnesses. (1984a, p. 81)

A unified truth that requires a plurality of consciousnesses reminds us that we can never be all knowing, all seeing, all understanding beings, but that we live in a vast chorus of humanity with the possibility to create, through its multiplicity of perspectives, what Bakhtin called "event potential." To believe otherwise is to destroy our potential for change and renewal. As he continues to interpret Bakhtin, Sidorkin asserts that he has not always believed that "the ideal of internal consistency of the self-concept may help destroy our dialogic potential" (1999, p. 65), but he has moved to that position. He explains:

> Up to a certain point in my life, I could relate to two completely opposite opinions and partly agree with both. I could talk to two mortal enemies blaming each other at different times, and feel solidarity with both of them. On the other hand, when somebody argues for a position that I share, there arises this urge to question it and find an argument against this very position. At the time, I believed this happened due to the lack of my own personal integrity. (p. 65)

As I read this, I was immensely relieved. Not only did someone understand; he shared my sense of confusion and angst. I could reconsider the issue of authenticity and integrity. I could better under-

stand Bakhtin's words that *"our conscious self* lives by its *unfinalizeability,* by its *unclosedness* and its *indeterminacy"* (1973, p. 53, italics mine). Unfinalizeability and unclosedness—I could resonate now, without fear of losing my moral compass, with his sense that

> when thought begins to work in an independent, experimenting and discriminating way, what first occurs is a separation between internally persuasive discourse and authoritarian enforced discourse. (1981d, p. 345)

The authoritarian voice of my parents and the church of my childhood began to break down as I listened to other voices. I became an independent thinker and began to voice my doubts, although I still seek answers to many questions. If God created life in such a way that homosexuality is not a choice, how could he then reject his creation? If as human beings, we share genetic make-up, how could inter-racial marriage be inherently wrong? If women are equal to men, why should I not open a door when I approach it? If intelligence is not fixed and test scores are not a predictor of any kind of success in life, if others learn in different ways and have different "intelligences," should I not expand and enlarge my understanding of "smart" and stop engaging in deficit thinking about others? I do not want to suggest that I held on to these particular prejudices until 1999, as that would be wrong; but there is no doubt that I, as we all do, held on to (and still hear) some authoritative voices whispering in my consciousness about my "moral turpitude." With Sidorkin I could say, "I was not alone in my inconsistency and that was good news" (p. 66).

The lesson is an important one for educators who need to learn that listening to an internal questioning and doubting dialogue is one manifestation of a dialogical moral self because "a fully consistent message simply does not capture the complexity of moral life" (Sidorkin, 2002, p. 156). I can resonate with the evils of child labor and still accept its value in helping children from poor families in developing countries to both stay alive and gain an educa tion. I can reject the lack of freedom that I would experience if forced to wear a burqa, but still permit Muslim women to make that choice for modesty for themselves, without decrying their decision as "archaic." I can talk with empathy with my Arab friend about the oppression of his people in Israel and also understand and condemn, as I talk to my Jewish friends, their fear and horror of suicide bombers and the need to overcome this threat. I can argue that it is important for all children to learn to a high academic standard and still reject the standardization that comes from norm-referenced tests. I can—and indeed—I must learn that my way is not *the* way, that American norms are not universal, and embrace the multiple voices inherent in diverse worldviews. I can, as a colleague once said, become suspicious whenever a sentence includes the words "*the* way. . .," immediately acknowledging there are multiple other ways authoritatively excluded by this very statement; and I can laugh at myself when I hear my voice offering in a meeting or with a friend, "well, we have three choices . . . !" because our choices are vast and generally much broader than we recognize or understand.

If one single voice is not capable of telling the truth and if a multitude of simultaneous voices is necessary for truth, then that same multitude of voices resounds in my inner dialogue, helping me to examine, re-examine, challenge, and modify my positions as appropriate. Sometimes this even requires representing a position we do not hold or even like in order for alternative perspectives to be brought into the conversation, in order to reject the paralysis of "groupthink" (Janis, 1982).

Often introducing a dissonant or dissenting position means that no quick or easy resolution will be achieved; hence, this is a difficult perspective to take. At the same time, it is one way for educators to open our minds and those of our students to the creation of new meanings and increased comprehension. It is also a concept that helps me to explain my discomfort with the position of some of my aca-

demic colleagues who argue for what they call an "affirmative action pedagogy," one that "seeks to bear witness to marginalized voices in our classrooms, even at the minor cost of limiting dominant voices" (Boler, 2004, p. 4). For me, and I think for Bakhtin and perhaps Sidorkin, the cost does not appear so minor.

If, in a class dealing with the current status of Indigenous peoples, we simply decry, as we ought, the persecution that occurred in many developed countries, including Australia, Canada, New Zealand, and the United States, we may feel comfortable in our disdain for the practices of earlier days. We may argue for the restoration of their lands, fishing, hunting, and mineral rights, and support their requests for compensation. However, unless we also introduce into the dialogue the perspectives of those whom new policies might impact—the logging companies, tourists, the landholders who will be displaced, we have only heard part of the story. We can argue for the restoration of the traditional whale hunt among Native Americans on the West coast, but unless we also hear the voices of scientists and conservationists, we are not dialogic. Bakhtin's reminder that the world is polyphonic and that we need to hear all voices rings in the back of my mind as a constant reminder.

In his 2002 book, Sidorkin picks up on this idea of including unpopular and oppositional voices, and says that, although "very few people are interested in hearing the terrorists' case" (p. 192), it is important to acknowledge evil in order to deal with it. He elaborates, saying that "this may strike one as a dangerous game to play: yet I maintain, all other strategies of dealing with evil are more dangerous" (p. 193). He explains that "prejudices spread and strengthen when their most outspoken bearers are marginalized and pushed outside the main public discourse" (p. 193). One wonders, for example, what implication this might have for those who protest the inclusion of world leaders such as Indonesian dictator Mohamed Suharto at international meet-

ings of leaders of OPEC countries and what impact having such a voice at the table might have on repressive national policies.

This is not easy. For educators, introducing unpopular or controversial positions into classroom discussions (even at upper secondary and university levels) can be risky. We may be critiqued and condemned by those who argue for fixed authoritative positions on any topic, but ultimately, rejecting certainty is a moral responsibility and representing multiple positions is an ethical act.

Bakhtin sums up this position as he states:

> The semantic structure of an internally persuasive discourse is not *finite*, it is *open*, in each of the new contexts that dialogize it, this discourse is able to reveal ever newer ways to *mean* . . . The process is made more complex by the fact that a variety of alien voices enter into the struggle for influence within an individual's consciousness. (1981d, pp. 346, 348)

Before we leave this discussion of inner dialogue and the moral life, it may be instructive to revisit Parker Palmer's work. We have seen that he has defined truth as impassioned and disciplined inquiry; yet, he states that

> community cannot take root in a divided life. Long before community assumes external shape and form, it must be present as seed in the undivided self: only as we are in communion with ourselves can we find community with others. (1998, pp. 89–90).

Some find in those words a position in direct opposition to the one we have been exploring through the work of Bakhtin. Although Bakhtin argues for lack of certainty, Palmer, in his apparent call for an undivided life, appears to argue the opposite. However, there is another way of interpreting Palmer that is totally consistent with the concept of an **unfinished dialogic self.** Palmer states that we must be in communion with ourselves. Another way to interpret this is to call for dialogue with ourselves if we are to be in community with others. We recall that Palmer has also stated that there "are no ultimate authori-

Unfinished dialogic self
refers to a person who lives as though there is always the possibility of being at least partially wrong

ties." Thus, we can interpret his words about the need to be in communion with ourselves to find community with others, as support for the dialogic nature of community which resides in our ability to conduct internal as well as external dialogue. In other words, when internal certainty and external openness come into conflict, we are divided; when we accept the moral dialogism in both spheres, community can emerge and develop.

We are in communion with our inner selves through dialogue, aware of the voices competing for attention. We no longer need to feel divided, concerned that a position that is less than irrevocable is wrong, torn apart over what seems to be the shifting of earlier acquired moral positions; instead, we are undivided in our sense of the dialogic self, in our belief that as we are open to our own inner voices, to the individual voices of others, and to the voices of the wider community (past and present), we will find "truth"—again in the small "t" sense of truth. Moreover, it is this openness, our awareness of ourselves as open, unfinished moral beings, which permits us to act morally and dialogically.

Acting Dialogically: A Temporary Finale

The inner dialogue of which we have been speaking, and the moral consciousness it produces, is not an end in itself. As we have seen before, dialogue is everything. But as we have also stated before, dialogue is not just words, not just talk, but an orientation to life and hence to action. Living dialogically is not a metaphor but a reality.

Bakhtin wrote:

> Dialog . . . is not the threshold to action, but the action itself. Nor is it a means of revealing, of exposing the already formed character of a person; no, here the person is not only outwardly manifested, he becomes for the first time that which he is, not only—we repeat—as far as others are concerned, but for himself as well. To be means to communicate dialogically. When the dialog is finished, all is finished. Therefore the dialog, in essence, cannot and must not come to an end. (1973, p. 213)

This connection between dialogue and life, between communicating dialogically and becoming who we really are (for others and for ourselves) is an ongoing, never finished process. Living in openness to others is life in its fullness; it permits us to make choices; to take positions; to act—in the fullness of our (albeit temporary) understandings of who we are. Likewise, and equally importantly, it does not imprison us in endless authoritative or relativist arguments.

I conclude this chapter about dialogue with a few additional comments about action—both to remain true to the complexity of Bakhtin's thinking and to serve as a reminder that dialogue is action. We live dialogically in the fullness of our humanity, informed by the humanity of many others who see life through different lenses—and then we act. Bakhtin clearly brings together the notion of dialogism with that of action when he writes:

> These voices are not self-enclosed or deaf to one another. They hear each other constantly, call back and forth to one another, and are reflected in one another (especially in the microdialogues). And outside this dialogue of 'conflicting truths' not a single essential act is realized, nor a single essential thought [expressed]. (1984a, p. 62)

Our actions become real, informed by the heteroglossia we have begun to perceive. As educators, for example, we might restrict the time we spend teaching to the test, and begin to recognize that there are many different standards, outcomes, and expressions of learning which require us to find numerous alternative ways for students to demonstrate what they have learned. Educators who adopt an ontological approach to dialogue as a way of life will constantly engage with others who are different from ourselves. We will question our positions and assumptions. We will be able to identify areas in which our prejudices about class or ethnicity result in deficit thinking and learn to reject the assumption that students whose home experiences are different from the dominant experiences are in some way deficient and inherently less able to learn. We will

never respond, as one teacher did when I asked her what it would take to help her students learn, "Better parents."

Living dialogically is not an excuse for not acting. There is no sense in a Bakhtinian worldview of paralyzing **relativism,** just as there is no room for **dogmatism.** Bakhtin actually considers these positions to be opposite ends of the same, unacceptable, continuum. He states,

> It is hardly necessary to mention that the polyphonic approach has nothing in common with relativism (nor with dogmatism). It should be noted that both relativism and dogmatism equally exclude all argumentation and all genuine dialog, either by making them unnecessary (relativism) or impossible (dogmatism). (1973, p. 56)

Standing in the midst of a heteroglossic world does not imply that we suspend judgment; it does not in any way suggest that every position is equally valid, equally right, or equally important. It does not imply that we should not try to understand and make determinations of desirable and undesirable, even right and wrong within given contexts. It simply implies that every perspective must be heard if we are to make valid judgments.

Often, those who come from deeply rooted religious positions find this notion unsettling. Some have deeply rooted beliefs and are convinced of their "rightness." The corollary must be that an opposing belief is "wrong." One way to deal with this conflict in a postmodern world is simply to accept a relativistic approach that says everyone is entitled to his or her own beliefs (correct) and that there is no point in discussing points of disagreements (incorrect). Dialogism leads to deeper understanding and to mutually respectful community.

Failing to explore and understand difference leads to individualism but also to a lack of tolerance. It increases fear and may lead, in the extreme to violence. If we accept an extreme postmodern position that everything is relative and there is no way to choose among perspectives, then, as Bakhtin states, argumentation is excluded. There is no further

Relativism

a philosophical theory suggesting that conceptions of truths and moral values are not absolute but relative to the persons or groups holding them

Dogmatism

the arrogant, stubborn assertion of opinion or belief that allows no opportunity for dialogue

need for dialogue or for interaction. One can simply live, believing in his or her perspective, closed to the voices of others because they have no value in a relativistic world.

In like fashion, if we are not open to polyphony, if we have already taken an authoritative voice as our own, if we are closed in our own dogmatism, there is also no need for dialogue—either as thought, words, or action. We live in a hermetically sealed shell oblivious to the world of "conflicting truths" around us. In a pluralistic, democratic society, taking a firm stance in favor of one set of beliefs or one position immediately precludes the possibility of dialogue. It sets up a hierarchy in which one person agrees to "tolerate" another, but inherently "lesser," position. This approach leads to exclusion and dominance, and ultimately precludes living meaningfully together in community.

Bakhtin is careful never to suggest that we can know nothing, or that there is no possibility of action. To the contrary he writes that "the starting point for understanding reality is the *present*" and that we should consciously base our understanding and action on "free *experience*" and on *"free imagination"* (1973, p. 88). We start where we are, learn to listen, and begin to understand. We speak freely, unfettered by society's norms and our emerging inner truths, so that we may express not only our convictions but also our doubts, fears, and disagreements. If we are to make valid decisions about appropriate courses of action, we do not permit inflexible, monologic, unexamined positions to constrain us. Hence, we start with the present, but never ignore the past because

> a dialogue of languages is a dialogue of social forces perceived not only in their static co-existence, but also as a dialogue of different times, epochs, and days, a dialogue that is forever dying, living, being born: co-existence and becoming are fused into an indissoluble concrete unity that is contradictory, multi-speeched and heterogeneous. (1981d, p. 365)

It is this contradictory but concrete unity that permits ideas to come to fruition, that permits us to move forward in educational institutions, never concerned about holding in tension conflicting perspectives, conflicting approaches, conflicting truths. We know that in this dialogue of past and present, people will come, having learned over time and throughout history, different ways of thinking about and perceiving the world. Holding these social forces and positions in tension permits us to move forward with increased understanding.

In a simplistic way, it is this reality that permits us to offer both whole language and phonics, without apology, not choosing between them, but recognizing that children learn in different ways and there is no "one best way" to learn. It is this concrete reality that permits us to offer bilingual programs, heritage language programs, English only programs, and English language learner programs in the same school or district—never as closed and bounded realities, but as ways of meeting children's needs as they live and learn together in a school community. It is the concrete multivocal reality that helps us understand the rationale for the creation of "full-service community schools" in which various community partners, parents, educators, and social service agencies come together to improve the coordination, delivery, effectiveness, and efficiency of services to children and families. All of this occurs because "the idea is a live event, played out at the point of dialogic meeting between two or several consciousnesses" (1984a, p. 88).

In 2004, Glass wrote, that

> moral *clarity* is not moral *certainty* but it still carries sufficient force to overcome relativist positions and orient liberatory practices that criticize or condemn oppression's surface appearances and deep structures. (p. 22, italics mine)

Seeking moral certainty precludes this kind of liber ation. However, the clarity that comes from living dialogically is unparalleled. It permits us to under stand more widely, more deeply, across time and

place, and to listen to the heteroglossia of life. In the next chapter, we will examine *carnival*, another of Bakhtin's key concepts, and one which permits us to move forward with clarity, to overcome some of the forces of oppression and to make positive changes in the ways in which we live and work.

GLOSSARY

Culture—expresses the customary beliefs, social norms, values, and material traits of a particular group of people. It is an integrated pattern of human behavior, thought, speech, action, and artifacts that determine what is acceptable or unacceptable. When we generalize these norms to expect certain behaviors from everyone in a group, we are using what are known as cultural stereotypes.

Dialogic interaction—not simply talk but the totality of the experience of an individual's contact with others with the implication that the individual is open to learning from that experience.

Dialogic relation—a way of relating to one another in the fullness of our existence and in the fullness of our differences. It is "extra-linguistic" in the sense that the debate about alternative perspectives is not simply words but embraces other ways of knowing, including the aesthetic, ethical, embodied, affective, or even erotic.

Dialogue—allows one to remain open to the Other, to difference, and to the possibility of new understandings. (See chapter 1)

Dogmatism—the arrogant, stubborn assertion of opinion or belief that, because there is no room for doubt or uncertainty, permits no opportunity for dialogue. One who expresses dogmatism is said to be dogmatic.

Exclusivity—implies that other perspectives, beliefs, and approaches are not valid in that the right or privilege claimed is only the domain of one group.

Inner dialogue—occurs when we permit a multitude of voices to help us examine, re-examine, challenge, and modify our positions as appropriate. It prevents the arrogance that often accompanies moral certainty.

Relationship—refers to our way of interacting with another, and primarily to whether we treat others as objects (it) or as subjects (animate beings) worthy of deep respect.

Relativism—a philosophical theory that conceptions of truth and moral values are not absolute but are relative to the persons or groups holding them. The corresponding adjective describing such thinking is relativistic.

Unfinished dialogic self—refers to someone who lives as though there is always the possibility of being wrong or at least partially wrong because there is always the possibility of learning something new.

NOTE

1   For many with a deep religious belief in a deity this is a difficult but important distinction. Nothing in what Bakhtin has said, or in my explanatory comments, is intended to suggest one should reject religious faith in order to live dialogically. However, I argue that when religious belief prevents openness and unfinishedness, when belief requires blind allegiance to a particular position, abrogating our responsibilities to be thinking, feeling human beings, then it might well be time to re-examine what we have come to understand our faith requires of us. For there is nothing in my personal religious conception of God that would cause me to be anything but open and loving to others.

Living in a Carnivalesque World

Bakhtin, in contrast to many of his contemporaries, does not simply suggest that we need to break out of our monological, authoritarian, hierarchical patterns of thinking and then leave us to try to figure out whether he has set us an impossible task. He actually introduces the concept of **carnival** as a way forward. Carnival, as Bakhtin conceptualizes it, certainly involves having fun, but it is much more than enjoying oneself. It is a way of breaking down barriers, of overcoming power inequities and hierarchies, of reforming and renewing relationships both personal and institutional.

Bakhtin's interpretation of carnival is particularly refreshing, because other approaches, such as Bourdieu's concept of *habitus* mentioned in Chapter 1, seem to leave us firmly entrenched in the status quo with little possibility of escaping the "structuring structures" and dispositions that constrain us. Others might argue that change is so difficult because we cannot overcome the structures and influences of power. Although Bakhtin does not often address

Carnival

a way of breaking down hierachical barriers and power inequities

power directly, it is clear that in his concept of carnival he finds a way of breaking out of the confines of tradition, hierarchy, and oppression, and of finding new, explicit, and more egalitarian ways of interacting. A "carnival sense of the world," according to Bakhtin, "possesses a mighty life-creating and transforming power, an indestructible vitality" (1984a, p. 107).

There is little doubt that Bakhtin is profoundly aware of the ways in which the typical organizational governance arrangements constrain us. They are not only hierarchical, but all-powerful, he says. However, Bakhtin does not spend time describing or analyzing oppression; instead, he focuses on the ways in which it may be temporarily overthrown. Moreover, although he reminds us repeatedly that carnival is impermanent in temporal terms, it is longer lasting in its effects. Once people have tasted liberty, it is difficult to return with acceptance to a former, more constrained state.

The carnival Bakhtin found so intriguing is not just any carnival. It is carnival that found its expression in medieval times, carnival that often persisted for days and weeks on end, permitting everyone to fully participate. Although some scholars trace the roots of carnival back to an old world European festival in about the tenth century AD, there does not seem to be a direct line between earlier celebrations and medieval carnival whose pre-Lenten celebrations incorporated many non-Christian practices and rituals. Sher (2002) writes that "Carnival from the 14th to the 16th century developed into one of the most important celebrations in Europe; so much so that by the 17th and 18th centuries the Church attempted to radically reform what was perceived to be an unmitigated adventure in sin and the pursuit of pleasure" (¶ 4). By the early nineteenth century, carnival had re-emerged as a celebration largely enjoyed by members of high society who "invested great sums in holding Carnival balls and masquerades" (¶ 4).

The evolution of carnival is important because Bakhtin sees in the concept of carnival, in more recent times, an erosion of some of the tenets he finds so appealing in medieval versions. "Beginning with the 17th century [the Renaissance] the folk carnival life begins to wane," he wrote, "It almost loses its quality of belonging to the whole people" (1973, p. 107). Carnival that belongs to the whole people is both planned and spontaneous; it is neither carefully orchestrated, nor organized in the common sense of the word. It might actually be correct to suggest that the carnival period itself is scheduled, but nothing within it is carefully structured or prescribed. Here, I choose a relatively long excerpt from the 1984 translation of the *Problems of Dostoevsky's Poetics* that outlines, in Bakhtin's own words, his understanding of carnival.

> Carnival is a pageant without footlights and without a division into performers and spectators. In carnival everyone is an active participant, everyone communes in the carnival act. Carnival is not contemplated, and, strictly speaking, not even performed; its participants *live* in it, they live by its laws as long as those laws are in effect; that is, they live a *carnivalistic life*. Because carnivalistic life is life drawn out of its *usual* rut, it is to some extent "life turned inside out," "the reverse side of the world" (*"monde à l'envers"*).
>
> The laws, prohibitions and restrictions that determine the system and order of ordinary, that is noncarnival, life are suspended during carnival: what is suspended first of all is hierarchical structure and all the forms of terror, reverence, piety, and etiquette connected with it—that is, everything resulting from socio-hierarchical inequality or any other form of inequality among people (including age). All *distance* between people is suspended, and a special carnival category goes into effect: *free and familiar contact among people.* This is a very important aspect of a carnival sense of the world. People who in life are separated by impenetrable hierarchical barriers enter into free familiar contact on the carnival square. (1984a, pp. 122–123)

We will return to the details of this passage later, but for now, we pause to consider what a different image of the world Bakhtin presents from that traditionally associated with institutional life, includ-

ing that experienced in educational organizations. Indeed, throughout this whole book, we have noted the newness and the richness of his vision. We live, not as prisoners of time, but in a time/space continuum that is dialogic, in which various historical, social, and cultural periods speak to one another, shaping current understandings and affecting the ways in which we understand the world. We experience the world, not through the eyes of historic or present, hierarchical, authoritative figures, but as polyphony—in all the excitement and complexity of heteroglossia. In addition, we have the ability to make choices—to live in an ontological dialogic orientation with the rest of the world, encountering and interacting with difference.

These images, though, are far from those which we, as educators, generally find in textbooks talking about accountability, data-driven decision making, curriculum alignment, resource allocation, instructional supervision, personnel administration, and so forth. Given their typical training which often focuses on "best practices" and pedagogical strategies, when educators encounter Bakhtin's notion of carnival, they generally raise their eyebrows, shake their head slightly, and wonder how anyone could imagine it applies to their daily routines. The mindset of carnival is just not on their horizon.

This attitude is not surprising considering how schooling as an institution has developed (at least in the western world) over the past centuries. The one-room schoolhouse gave way to large buildings of brick and mortar, too frequently resembling the factories, hospitals, and prisons that were built at the same time. Even today, new school buildings tend to be more like these other institutions than like the imaginative office buildings and museums that have been architecturally designed and carefully erected in many cities. However, and this is fortunate for most of us, although we cannot make major changes to the physical structures in which we work, we can definitely approach our work differently, informed by Bakhtin's innovative approach to life.

Carnival: A Joyous and Participatory Approach to Life

Carnival is not a spectator sport. It is not something one watches (as in a show with footlights); it is a life one lives—temporarily but vibrantly. This is so important to Bakhtin that he uses almost the same words to introduce the concept in his discussion of Dostoevsky (above) as he did in his dissertation about Rabelais, where he wrote:

> Carnival does not know footlights, in the sense that it does not acknowledge any distinction between actors and spectators. . . . Carnival is not a spectacle seen by the people; they live in it, and everyone participates because its very idea embraces all the people. While carnival lasts, there is no other life outside it. (1984b, p. 7)

Having the opportunity to live a carnivalesque life on a temporary basis offers the possibility of new norms, new approaches to the normal routines of non-carnival daily life. Carnival, Bakhtin tells us, is life turned upside down and inside out. Nothing resembles the normal experience, nothing is predictable; the rules change and nothing is the same.

Here, Bakhtin explicitly addresses the hierarchy and power that constrain so much of human life, that result in some people being marginalized while others are accepted, some being included while others are excluded, some being oppressed and others privileged, some voices being heard and others silenced. In carnival, Bakhtin tells us, the first aspect of life that is suspended is the hierarchical structures that determine our "proper" place—including the acceptable ways of talking, dressing, laughing, and celebrating. Everything, he claims, that is associated with socio-hierarchical inequality or any other form of inequality—including fear, awe, holiness, and good manners—is suspended. There is no doubt that this is a somewhat idealized view of carnival, yet Bakhtin would likely argue that in medieval times, carnival as lived out in the public square was exactly that— a time and a place—an event in which the world was turned upside down and those who were nor-

mally separated by hierarchical barriers entered into free and unrestrained contact.

It may well be useful here to take time to recall the importance of the ancient public square, the agora as it was called in Greece, or the forum in ancient Rome. The agora was the "heart of ancient Athens, the focus of political, commercial, administrative and social activity, the religious and cultural centre, and the seat of justice" (Hellenic Ministry of Culture, 2001). It was, in both ancient Greece and ancient Rome, a square area in a readily accessible part of the city, open to all—an area often surrounded by major public buildings such as the royal palace, the law courts, the assembly house, and the jail. In other words, the public square was a place where people gathered without sanction or restraint to witness all of the important events of daily life, to debate them, and to conduct business. Today the term *agora* has been widely adopted by groups in several countries, emphasizing the role of public debate in such diverse situations as "digital democracy" or "global online research in agriculture." It is also the name of many publications and Web search programs including one sponsored by the government of France (see Agora, 2005). In each, *agora* reminds us that the processes are open to everyone, that participation is the basis of success.

Bakhtin takes pains to analyze the conditions that permit such an amazing inversion to occur, focusing on the ways in which carnival creates a new mode of interrelationship among those who participate. He discusses:

Grotesque
according to Bakhtin refers to natural forms and monstrous figures intertwined in bizarre and fanciful ways

- the notion of carnival misalliances which may offer possibilities for the re-creation of boundaries,
- the function of eccentricity and the **grotesque** which empowers the use of language, including profanation (which permits new forms of communication),

Mask
refers not only to physical masks but also to metaphorical ones

- the use of **masks** and marionettes (that enables us to present multiple personae and to overcome fear),

- ritual acts such as fire or the mock crowning and uncrowning of the carnival king,

Parody

a way of imitating someone in a satirical or humorous way

- the role of laughter including **parody,** and finally,
- the role of opposites including death and birth as symbols of regeneration.

The foregoing represent profoundly and inherently interconnected and interrelated elements of carnival. We shall explore each in turn as a way of thinking about the possibility of carnival in schools. First, though, to ensure we have some sense of what he might be talking about, let me suggest several carnival-like occurrences with which we are quite familiar in schools.

Some schools introduce special dress-up days in which everyone is encouraged to wear pajamas or Hawaiian or flapper garb and so forth. Others enjoy regular sports competitions in which staff play against students or sometimes staff and students play on the same team against a team from an opposing school or "house." In some schools, there is a day in which students become "teachers for the day," and teachers sit in students' seats. One school I know begins the year with a mini-golf game played along the school's corridors. Another has a group of teachers take all new eighth-graders to a three-day camp. Still another has teachers work together on a "ropes" course. Homecoming festivals, Halloween parties, and so forth can all serve to bring to mind events to which Bakhtin's comments might apply and which might be enriched by a deeper, more thorough understanding of the aspects of carnival that seem pertinent to him. These constitute but a starting point for understanding Bakhtin's *carnival.*

New Modes of Relationship

Bakhtin examines how new structures, relationships, and patterns of communication arise from the old forms of institutional life. He is convinced that this does not happen through punishment or sanction of individuals who have engaged in what one perceives to be inequitable or uncaring practices or even through the application of rules. Instead,

Bakhtin's approach is that experiencing new ways of being helps people to see alternatives of possibility and justice. Bakhtin states,

> Carnival is the place for working out, in a concretely sensuous, half-real and half-play acted form, *a new mode of interrelationship between individuals,* counterposed to the all-powerful socio-hierarchical relationships of non-carnival life. (1984a, p. 123)

During carnival, the only laws that operate are the laws of "freedom" as all others are temporarily suspended. Thus, students can take on the role of teachers; parents can rub shoulders with teachers; and principal, superintendent, and directors of education can participate alongside one another.

Carnival, Bakhtin, argues, changes existing patterns and overthrows hierarchies. It is not like the "official feasts of the Middle Ages" (1984b, p. 9) or like many of our holiday celebrations today that reinforce established hierarchies and their existing "religious, political and moral values" (p. 9). Carnival is not the official pageantry that accompanies the inauguration of a president or other high ranking public official; it is not the kind of celebration one sees during the installation of a newly elected pope. On a more mundane level, Bakhtin is not talking about the kinds of celebrations in schools in which some students are rewarded for specific achievements, while other students are excluded from the celebrations. This is not what Bakhtin means by "carnival"; rather his carnival is raucous, unpredictable, and inclusive. There was no formality, no prepared speeches, and no decorum in the temporary state Bakhtin called carnival. In carnivalesque celebrations, no principal or teacher is exempt from a slap on the back, a pie in the face, a dunk in the tank—or whatever normally disrespectful activity best expresses the spirit of the day. In real carnival, there is no rank, no privilege. Indeed, Bakhtin clarifies:

> As opposed to the official feast, one might say that carnival celebrated temporary liberation from the prevailing truth and from the established order; it marked the suspension of all hierarchical rank,

> privileges, norms, and prohibitions. Carnival was the true feast of time, the feast of becoming, change, and renewal. It was hostile to all that was immortalized and completed. (p. 10)

Bakhtin repeats his statement about carnival being a temporary suspension of hierarchy only a few pages later, and then adds that in carnival, a "real type of communication, impossible in ordinary life, is established" (p. 16). These new modes of communication "offer the chance to have a new outlook on the world, to realize the relative nature of all that exists, and to enter a completely new order of things" (p. 34). They permit us to express ourselves differently than we might in normal everyday conversation or discourse and they afford the opportunity to interact with those with whom we rarely, if ever, come into contact.

This opportunity for "carnival misalliances" is one of the ways in which boundaries may be overturned and re-created. In carnival, especially if wearing masks, the jester and the king interact as equals, the lawyer and the accused are indistinguishable. In carnivalesque moments in a school, the student, teacher, and administrator come together to enjoy a temporary suspension of the rules and routine and to work together to build the best possible sand castle or ice sculpture, and so forth. The outstanding academically oriented, college-bound student and the one who is failing in all subjects and is on the verge of dropping out are united in their quest for points for their team in order to compel their teacher to follow through on a promise of dying her hair or of buying pizza for the whole class. Because their academic histories, their family backgrounds, or their reputations are irrelevant in the suspended world of carnival, new relationships may be formed in what Bakhtin calls "the living *present*" (1984a, p. 108). The players do not have to speak or act in guarded, artificial ways that preserve the identities they have carefully constructed—or that have been constructed by others and imposed on them—over time; instead, they are able to "act and speak in a zone of familiar con-

tact with the open-ended present . . . to *consciously* rely on *experience* (to be sure, as yet insufficiently mature) and on *free invention*" (p. 108). For the moment, neither the academic grades nor the looming deadline for college admission, nor the need to find well-paying employment are forefront in their minds. The carnivalesque task of the present takes precedence and unites them in a new mode of inter-relationship.

Here it is important to re-emphasize a point Bakhtin makes repeatedly: carnival is temporary. Suspension of rules and roles is temporary. Indeed, even within carnivalesque activities there may be moments when roles and hierarchies reemerge. If a teacher sees a child engaging in unsafe behavior, the adult sense of responsibility overrules (and should overrule) the excitement of the competition. There may, however, be subtle changes as people interact with one another in new ways and the change persists long after the carnivalesque activity itself ends.

The Function of Eccentricity and the Grotesque

In carnival, a kind of eccentricity permits "the latent sides of human nature to reveal and express themselves" (1984a, p. 123). We do not have to bite our tongue, repress our thoughts, or clench our fists in an earnest attempt to stifle our attitudes, but instead we may find ways to express our true feelings, to communicate who we are and what we are about—not in ways that are destructive but in ways that permit us to discover our true humanity as we are able to express ourselves in the fullness of the moment. We do not take advantage of this opportunity in a way that leaves us vulnerable. Instead, we enter into the joyous mood of carnival, enjoying the costumes, masks, and grotesque representations—and under their cover, we seize the opportunity for free expression.

Here it is critically important to understand what Bakhtin means by the *grotesque* because it differs from the ways in which we often use the term. For Bakhtin, the term is related to artistic conceptions of the world, to the combination of "natural forms and monstrous figures intertwined in bizarre or fanciful" ways (*American Heritage Dictionary,* 2000). He does not use the term as a form of social commentary. In his discussion of Rabelais and his world, Bakhtin takes pains to discuss the concept of the grotesque presented by a contemporary German art critic named Kayser in a book whose title translates as *The Grotesque in Painting and Art* (published posthumously in 1957; see Bakhtin 1984b, pp. 46–52). Bakhtin is concerned about the modern tendency to make of the grotesque something static, "hostile, alien, and inhuman" (p. 47). In this modernist construction, the grotesque becomes alienating and alienated from real life.

Bakhtin rejects the notion of the grotesque as something strange or foreign in part because it leaves "no room for the material bodily principle with its inexhaustible wealth and perpetual renewal" (1984b, p. 48). Instead, he argues for making the grotesque an integral part of everyday life, for neither ignoring nor glossing over it. In the world of carnival presented by Rabelais (and endorsed by Bakhtin), bodily functions, for example, figure prominently in the humor, the parodies, and the profanities of carnival. Thus, when we accept the grotesque as yet another part of real life, exercise our freedom from societal constraints, and choose to bring the body into the life of carnival, there is a strange kind of empowerment. Bakhtin uses as an illustration the images of death as "a more or less funny monstrosity" which appear in medieval and Renaissance paintings such as those of Holbein (pp. 50–51). He states that in subsequent years, people "forgot the principle of laughter presented in macabre images" which then became "interpreted in an unrelieved, serious aspect and became flat and distorted" (p. 51). For Bakhtin, death is a natural part of life and should be treated as such. For him, therefore, the grotesque is a way of making natural what often seems unnatural and of finding in the ability to mock the grotesque a means for overcoming fear and distaste, for gener-

ating renewal and rebirth.

This is a difficult concept for educators. In one way, Bakhtin's concept implies the need to build on all of life's experiences and realities and to permit them to become fodder for conversation and exploration in a classroom. Within the parameters of what is appropriate for a specific group of students (based on age, maturity, cultural norms and the like), one might want to help students to think about what we commonly reject as grotesque, as ugly, or undesirable—either in daily living or as subjects which may be brought into the curriculum.

For some educators and students, it might be necessary to confront the presence of illness or death, permitting students who are facing the loss of a loved one to bring the realities of their experience to the classroom discussions. For others, this might constitute an examination of the nature of grinding poverty. Although one might well equate living in rat and roach infested tenements with bathroom facilities shared among several families and bare light bulbs hanging from the ceiling for evening illumination with the "grotesque"; moreover, it does not mean these conditions should be ignored, nor the voices of students living in such conditions, silenced. These students might not be able to write a descriptive paragraph for a standardized test about a ski vacation in the Rockies, but they could talk and write intelligently about the challenges of crowded and substandard urban living. In other words, their form of "normal" should not be rejected in favor of more middle-class conceptions of reality and normality.

For others, the "grotesque" might take quite a different form, represented by huge mansions, gilt decorated swimming pools, and lavish expenditures on the part of those who apparently live in ignorance of their impoverished neighbors. The point is that, rather than remain silent about the range of human conditions, children must be encouraged to discuss their lived realities without shame or fear of reprisals; more importantly, they need to be able to build on what they know in order to achieve school success, whether what they know is in another's eyes "grotesque" or not. It is therefore important to acknowledge the existence of the "grotesque," to explore its forms, and to understand how such explorations can lead to the possibility of change and rebirth through the creation of new understandings and more inclusive practices.

For Bakhtin, the grotesque is profoundly connected to real life. "The last thing one can say of the grotesque," he argued, "is that it is static; on the contrary it seeks to grasp in its imagery the very act of becoming and growth, the eternal incomplete unfinished nature of being" (p. 52). What appears grotesque in one time and place is different from the grotesque in another space or another era. Here the notion of chronotope comes back into play. For that reason, including both playful, artistic conceptions of grotesque, and more disturbing real-life notions in the curriculum are important. When we learn to integrate the grotesque, the ugly, the unspeakable—however defined and conceptualized—into the content of our lessons, into the fabric of schooling, we overcome the tendency to ignore it, and acknowledge once again, the possibility of change.

As Bakhtin wrote about it, incorporating the grotesque into carnival has the ability to teach us not to take ourselves too seriously, not to avoid talking about normal bodily functions. Of particular importance for educators, it gives permission for children to bring all of their life's experiences to the learning situation.

The Use of Language

The ability to temporarily suspend hierarchies and social conventions also created,

during carnival time a special type of communication impossible in everyday life. This led to the creation of special forms of marketplace speech and gesture, frank and free, permitting no distance between those who came in contact with each other and liberating from norms of etiquette and decency imposed at other times. (1984b, p. 10)

Some new forms of communication as elaborated by Bakhtin may sound rude and inappropriate to those outside the interaction, but Bakhtin assures us they have special meaning to those who use them. Bakhtin says,

> For instance when two persons establish friendly relations, the form of their verbal intercourse also changes abruptly; they address each other informally, abusive words are used affectionately, and mutual mockery is permitted. (p. 16)

At first this may sound unlikely, but consider your relationship with your best friend. Just today, I engaged in an exchange which, taken out of context, would be totally misinterpreted. Having been out of touch for several days while we both traveled during a recent holiday period, we had missed each other's phone calls. Upon receiving an email message stating, "Sorry to have missed you, I'll try again tomorrow," my immediate response (also by email) was "If you don't, I'll shoot you." In like fashion, think about the use of slang and even of racial epithets by good friends who are likely to affectionately call each other "girlfriend" or "Nigger"–contrary to all accepted conventions outside of a close relationship and within the spirit of carnivalesque liberation and joyful abandon. Seeing one adult male make what is generally accepted to be a lewd finger gesture might leave an unknowing observer wondering how one person could be so rude to another without provoking an angry response. However, from within a close relationship, the gesture takes on a different meaning. The utterance becomes an affectionate form of refuting what the other has said, perhaps even of teasingly acknowledging that a good point has been made in the casual repartee of the relationship. Thus, in some ways, one can appreciate how relationship may develop, over time, some carnivalesque elements. Such exchanges are not necessarily the norm. They do not constitute everyday or public occurrences, but they are part of the fabric of exchanges and interactions which constitute the whole. In like fashion, relations within organiza-

tions need an element of carnival, of fun, of mockery, and of the unexpected in order to promote the kinds of exchanges that evoke creativity and liberation.

Bakhtin identifies abusive language, profanities, and oaths and general marketplace speech as characteristic of new forms of communication made possible in times of carnival. The carnival spirit transformed their "primitive verbal functions, acquired a general tone of laughter, and became, as it were, so many sparks of the carnival bonfire which renews the world" (p. 17). Educators, sometimes convinced of the need to become both language and thought police, are often appalled when a student uses what the teacher generally considers to be inappropriate or excessively familiar language, and may exercise discipline rather than respond lightly in kind. Hence, the possibility of a linguistic exchange that might deflect the seriousness of a situation or prevent its escalation into full blown conflict is sometimes lost in the failure to permit a carnivalesque moment to develop.

I recall a time when, as a very young substitute teacher, wearing (as was stylish in those days) a relatively short hot-pant outfit, I walked into the classroom of an absent secondary school history teacher. To my amazement, I was confronted with a class comprised of 20 young men and only a few girls. More surprisingly, I had learned, just prior to entering the classroom, that there were no female teachers on the staff. Given the normal male culture of the school, a somewhat carnivalesque atmosphere was immediately created in that classroom by the appearance of a young female teacher. Many of the boys immediately tried to establish a rapport through what could only be perceived as cat-calls and suggestive comments. There was (and is still) no doubt in my mind that their behavior was inappropriate in that it was both sexist and objectifying. At the same time, fortunately, my professionalism took over, and I refrained from anger. I was able to perceive that the young men were trying, although inappropriately, to establish a relationship with me using the means

with which they were familiar in their daily lives. I responded in ways suggestive of a brief carnivalesque repartee and then suggested we get down to work. Had I taken offense, expressed outrage at their comments, bristled, or tried to discipline the "offenders," I might never have succeeded in overcoming their initial surprise and in completing the lesson plan for the day. The brief interlude was supplanted by a serious consideration of the topic at hand.

In another setting, I might have moved the conversation in a different direction, focusing on the ways in which men can objectify women and vice versa, talking about appropriate ways to express admiration, exploring how sexism has resulted in misunderstanding and sometimes oppression in society. However, in this instance, my goal was to establish a pedagogical relation with the students—one that would permit me to complete the objective of the lesson. For that purpose, permitting a brief moment of carnival, in which rules were suspended, served me well.

Bakhtin asserts that characteristic of carnival is "a naked posing of ultimate questions on life and death" (1984a, p. 134), but it does not permit one to find an "abstractly philosophical or religiously dogmatic resolution; it plays them out in the concretely sensuous form of carnivalistic acts and images" (p. 134). The language and topics of carnival are uncensored. There are no taboo topics, no ideas that cannot be explored.

A ninth-grade student was instrumental in teaching me this lesson. Courtenay was a slight, fair haired, bright, and mischievous boy who was irrepressible in his comments during class. He also suffered from cystic fibrosis and, during his ninth-grade year, after a short period of hospitalization, he died. During the fall, however, he begged to be permitted to participate in the school debating club and traveled with us to several tournaments. His willingness to endure the challenges of his illness, to talk openly about his condition with his friends, and his somewhat irreverent approach to life both endeared him to and separated him from the others. As his illness progressed and his death approached, Courtenay became truant more and more often. He had too many things to do, people to see, to sit confined at a desk in the classroom. He and his parents asked me to talk about his situation with his classmates to help them to understand that Courtenay had competing needs, but that when he was in school, it was because he wanted to socialize with his friends; academic achievement was far from a priority. I had not been trained to meet Courtenay's needs and I certainly had never considered how to have such conversations with ninth grade students. However, as I talked with them about life and death, about priorities and choices, powerful learning took place. Although the topic of death is not one usually associated with carnival, it is one which Bakhtin says is inherently present. Death is part of life and therefore must be discussed naturally; further, when we are successful, the discussion can bring a kind of carnivalesque release. This was not a theoretical discussion of life and death, but acknowledgment of the experiences and needs of a classmate. How much better to explore them openly than to have made of them mysteries or taboos!

Although carnival is but a temporary phenomenon, the ability to engage with other students and teachers in discussion of the whole range of human activity can be both liberating and informative. I sometimes wonder when I read stories in the media of a teacher denying a kindergarten child the possibility of folding hands and saying a quiet prayer of thanks before eating a snack, or of school administrators refusing to permit the creation of a club for gay and lesbian students, how we can teach students to accept diversity in our society if educators repress and silence such important aspects of human life.

I am reminded of a very simple example. One time when I was working as a secondary school teacher, a colleague came to me to complain about the impertinent questions two girls in my homeroom class had asked her. Curious, I asked for more information.

It appeared that she had been assigned to supervise a student teacher-intern who was at the point in the process when she was to be left alone in charge of a class. When my students (legitimately I thought) asked if their teacher still got paid when there was an intern in charge of the class, she bristled with indignation. Why was she so closed to outsided-ness, to the open and honest questions of her students? Why was she so predisposed to believe their question was an insult? When educators have some experience with the language and experiences of carnival and believe that the whole range of experience is a legitimate basis for learning, they are much less likely to take offense at honest but direct questions posed even after the carnival period has passed.

The Use of Masks and Marionettes

The symbolism of masks is certainly ambivalent. People wear masks to disguise what are not always benevolent intents; sometimes criminals wear masks to prevent their identification. Sometimes, one puts on a figurative mask to hide feelings of insecurity, hurt, or confusion that one hopes to conceal from those around them. Throughout the ages and across many cultures and civilizations, masks hold an unquestioned fascination. Bakhtin calls the mask the "most complex theme of folk culture" (1984b, p. 39).

The mask permits one to struggle against conventions, against all that oppresses or marginalizes or disempowers because it provides the possibility of liberation and new identity. Masks, Bakhtin states, "in the struggle against conventions, and against the inadequacy of all available life-slots to fit an authentic human being" take on an "extraordinary significance" (1981c, p. 163):

> They grant the right *not* to understand, the right to confuse, to tease, to hyperbolize life; the right to parody others while talking, the right to not be taken literally, not "to be oneself," the right to life in the chronotope of the entr'acte. (p. 163)

The theme of freedom and liberation that runs

through Bakhtin's depiction of carnival is ever present in his concept of masks, in which, when we take on a new persona, we are free from the pressures of the identities we have constructed for ourselves. The use of masks provides a time when we actually can construct our own identity rather than having others construct it for us as the shop keeper did for Amita in Chapter 3. It offers us the ability to reflect on who we are and how we want to present ourselves (even figuratively) to the world. We are free to admit our ignorance; it is all right not to know or understand. We are free to admit to confusion, to discover the tensions and paradoxes of life that prevent knowing with absolute certainty. We are free to become "other" than the one we have so far presented as our "public persona" or as others expect us to be. In carnivalesque situations, we may choose to wear the mask of an emperor or empress from a previous era to emphasize our sense of power. We may select the mask of an animal to suggest stealth, slyness, quickness or conversely, to emphasize shyness and a desire to hide and not be noticed.

As students prepare for a theatrical production, for example, they take on new roles. Not only do the actors acquire stage personas, but the young woman who seemed so unsure of herself in class becomes an extroverted prima donna on stage; the young man who responded so tentatively demonstrates his considerable ability with tools and design and constructs the most amazing stage sets. The stutterer comes to life as he is able to communicate using his rich baritone in the annual musical. His posture changes and he no longer seems to fold in on himself. The mask is, therefore, both literal and figurative.

When one puts on a literal mask, one has the option of choosing a new identity, of changing one's image and sense of self. One can playfully become a ruler, an infamous celebrity, or an animal. The opportunities are endless and one can engage in a totally new relationship with another also wearing a mask without anyone ever being any the wiser. To

rub shoulders playfully with someone against whom one has held a grudge for several years may be the beginning of a resolution to the conflict. To develop a new relationship as Maid Marion to another's Robin Hood or as Rhett Butler to another's Scarlett O'Hara is to discover, not only some of the hidden dreams of another, but to take on a new identity through a new relationship, perhaps in a different historic or cultural context.

Bakhtin concludes his description of masks with the statement that they give us the "right to betray to the public a personal life, down to its most private and prurient little secrets" (p. 163). Here he is not necessarily advocating that we "tell all" but assuring us that, during carnival, as we take on masks and new identities, we need not fear who we are. It is permissible to relax and be ourselves, no longer needing to live in guarded and self-censoring ways. This is because, Bakhtin asserts,

> The mask is connected with the joy of change and reincarnation, with gay relativity and with the merry negation of uniformity and similarity; it rejects conformity to oneself. The mask is related to transition, metamorphoses, the violation of natural boundaries, to mockery, and familiar nicknames. It contains the playful element of life; it is based on a peculiar interrelation of reality and image, characteristic of the most ancient rituals and spectacles. (1984b, pp. 39–40)

Bakhtin contrasts this version of a mask with one that later developed during the "Romantic period" in which the mask takes on new and alien meanings; it "hides something, keeps a secret, deceives . . . [it] loses its regenerating and renewing element and acquires a somber hue" (p. 40).

Bakhtin is sometimes critiqued for an unduly optimistic and simplistic vision of carnival. Hence, it is important to recognize that Bakhtin acknowledges the negative side of carnival and of its accoutrements such as masks. His is not simplistic, rather organic—a way of thinking that recognizes the deep interconnections of life in which joy is not separated from sorrow, love from hate, death from life, peace from uproar, and so forth. His is a world in which regeneration, change, and renewal are always possible, in which from the ashes of one form, another more vibrant may rise. Thus, for Bakhtin, the mask is a symbol of all that is possible in the moments of true carnival in the lives of individuals, interpersonal relationships, or of institutional life. Joyful and optimistic carnival does not discount the possibility and presence of evil; it simply provides a way to move forward.

Masks during a time of carnival permit one to say what one fears to admit in the ordinary routine of institutional life. But once the principal, or school superintendent, or chair of the school board has heard a frank (albeit concealed) critique of the new literacy program during a gala costume ball, the idea has been released and begs consideration and reflection. Hence, masks help us to acknowledge some of the problems as well as new possibilities that exist in institutional life. They also help us to acknowledge that we have multiple identities, numerous facets, and personae.

We can and must make choices regarding who we want to become, how we want others to construct us, and how we want to engage with others in new ways. We do not need to be confined by fear of what others think or be concerned that our hesitant steps toward self-recreation may fail because we have the moments of carnival in which to take our tentative first steps.

For educators, it becomes imperative to find ways, even though fleeting and transitory, to permit students to take on different personalities, different realities and to do so through the wonderfully creative and freeing vehicle of the mask. A language arts teacher might provide simple craft material, sticks, (or even long pencils), and encourage students to make masks representing a character in a play or novel and to act out a particular situation as though they were the characters come to life in the modern world. Alternatively, they might make marionettes rather than masks, expressing similar real-

ities. A biology teacher might encourage students to take on the identity of an animal, learning about life and love from an alternative perspective; (the amazing popularity of movies such as *The March of the Penguins* might make this a popular and informative activity for many students). Imagine helping teenage boys to express the emotional reaction of a father penguin that has through sleet and storm protected the egg and the newborn chick only to find it has not survived the trek with its mother back to the sea. In so doing, the subtle message about the validity of emotions may be safely communicated to male teenage students and be equally safely received by them.

Masks as symbols of otherness, of change, and renewal provide the opportunity to explore interactions with those from other cultures, other socio-economic backgrounds, from different religious perspectives, as well as to delve deep within to better understand oneself.

Ritual Acts Such as Crowning and Uncrowning of Carnival Rulers

One sometimes hears questions being raised by educators and parents about the value of traditions such as homecoming with its crowning of a king and queen. The justifiable concern is about the **elitism** and the exclusivity of the practice. However, if the selection were done by a lottery instead of a vote, and the position were open to all students, could the experience provide a carnivalesque moment in the Bakhtinian sense, overturning the traditional perceptions of popularity and power in a school?

Following the devastation of Hurricane Katrina in 2005, there were frequent acerbic debates conducted through the media about whether New Orleans should cancel Mardi Gras and focus its attention on reconstruction. I can only suspect Bakhtin might have agreed with the decision to go ahead with the carnival celebration. What Bakhtin might say to those advocating a cessation of carnival is that it is an act of renewal, essential in times of tragedy and dislocation because of the hope it offers

Elitism
the belief that certain persons or members of certain groups deserve favored treatment by virtue of their perceived superiority

and its temporary relief from the sadness and sorrow of the reconstructive efforts.

Bakhtin writes extensively about crowning and uncrowning as important symbolic rituals in his discussion of Dostoevsky's novel. He calls it the "primary carnivalistic act" (1984a, p. 124). Moreover, it is a ritual carried out in numerous contexts throughout the world—from the crowning of the Mardi Gras king, to the choice of a new pope or the formal induction of a new monarch; from the former popular television show "Queen for a Day" to the now popular crowning of winners of the omnipresent reality shows, and to the annual banquets and celebrations of so many service clubs and volunteer organizations—crowning of victors or leaders is a hotly contested and highly prized activity. For Bakhtin, what is particularly important about this ritual act is that

> crowning/decrowning is a dualist ambivalent ritual, expressing the inevitability and at the same time the creative power of the shift-and-renewal, the *joyful relativity* of all structure and order, of all authority and all (hierarchical) position. Crowning already contains the idea of immanent decrowning . . . The ritual of decrowning completes, as it were, the coronation and is inseparable from it . . . Carnival celebrates the shift itself, the very process of replaceability . . . (pp. 124–125).

Bakhtin suggests that ritual acts remind us that both individuals and structures are relative and transitory. In the inauguration ceremony for a new American president, one is always aware that a new election will occur in four years; so the ritual reminds us that the incumbent's power is always temporary. Bakhtin, though, goes further. He argues that carnival and its ritual acts are reminders that structures themselves are also relative and transitory. This is a more difficult concept to grasp, for we often decry the slowness of systems to change. At the same time, the Roman or British Empires, the terrifying reigns of Robespierre or Ivan the Terrible, the extensive conquests of Caesar, Napoleon, the conquistadors; the tyranny of slavery in the United States—all have

come to an end. This does not, of course, deny the persistence of their influence in the often unequal structures and systems that have replaced them, for to deny the ongoing influence and persistence of unequal power relations would be to ignore the chronotope connections between past and present. At the same time, change does and can occur.

In education, the ritual carnivalesque acts may be less obvious, but exist nonetheless. A new reading or science program may be introduced with great fanfare, new books for students, instructional materials for every classroom, and professional development workshops for teachers. For those who have opposed the choice, perhaps because it seems decontextualized and inauthentic, there is hope in the reminder that such pedagogic structures are temporary. In like fashion, the election of a new school board, or the choice of a new principal, although welcomed by some, may be critiqued by others.

For Bakhtin an encouraging aspect of carnival is its reminder that the power evident in so many organizational structures—the installation of kings, powerful rulers, and hierarchical leaders, or even the introduction of new programs or reform efforts—has limits and will come to an end. Oppression, too, can be overthrown, challenged, transformed.

The Role of Laughter

In part it is the laughter that arises during the mock crowning of a symbolic and temporary ruler that offers the hope of a new future. The mocking seriousness of the swearing in of a royal court to support and attend to the ruler, all the while joking and teasing and poking fun at the one they are swearing to support and whose power they are taking oaths to uphold is one way of suggesting the power each individual has to overcome oppression. Laughing at ourselves, at the situation at hand, and at others is one way of becoming aware of our own agency. We do not have to be passive, unhappy by-standers; but can instead become active, joyful participants in the carnival of life.

> Enormous creative, and therefore genre-shaping, power was possessed by ambivalent carnivalistic laughter. This laughter could grasp and comprehend a phenomenon in the process of change and transition. (1984a, p. 164)

One strength of this laughter, as we have seen with other elements, is its ability to hold multiple and contradictory elements in tension. It does not permit elements to be either "absolutized or to congeal in one-sided seriousness" (p. 164). Carnivalesque laughter excludes all one-sidedness and dogmatism. It is not an "individual reaction to some isolated 'comic' event" but rather a "festive laughter" (1984b, p. 11). It is "universal in scope" directed at everyone and no one, and it is "ambivalent," gay and triumphant.

Bakhtin argued that one of the most important aspects of this festive laughter was that it was not directed only at a target in some sort of mean-spirited mockery, but at those who laugh as well. It embraced everyone, included everyone and denied no-one and nothing and hence held within it the possibility of regeneration. Nothing was sacred; everything could be subjected to its gaze and derision, ambiguous derision to be sure.

Moreover, laughter makes possible a gaze that is both probing and complete; it permits one to see much more than can normally be perceived through the guarded filters of daily life. In North American culture, one evidence of this is the ongoing popularity of such television features as David Letterman's top 10 lists, *The Daily Show* with John Stewart, or Jay Leno's opening monologue which often addresses topics from current events. Such programs use laughter to make fun of institutions, individuals, and political processes, and at the same time, offer a serious critique.

In some ways, we draw back, looking away from much of life, either fearing what we may see and learn about ourselves, or disliking what we notice about the world around us with its injustice and inequity. Indeed, too often we refuse to look, and hence, often ignore the beauty and vibrancy of everyday life.

What we see depends on where we stand or sit. We are too often constrained by our culture, our status, our position and, therefore, we fail to see clearly. Laughter, on the other hand, has

> the remarkable power of making an object come up close, of drawing it into a zone of crude contact where one can finger it familiarly on all sides, turn it upside down, inside out, peer at it from above and below, break open its external shell, look into its center, doubt it, take it apart, dismember it, lay it bare and expose it, examine it freely and experiment with it. Laughter demolishes fear and piety before an object, before a world, making of it an object of familiar contact and thus clearing the ground for an absolutely free investigation of it. (1981a, p. 23)

What an amazing description of the power of laughter—and what a solid argument for introducing some fun, enjoyment, carnivalesque moments into the daily and weekly routines of our classrooms. When we permit laughter to reign, there is a freedom which permits exploration and learning to occur. We are consumed with curiosity, set aside preconceived ideas, lose our fear of not being able to master a new topic, and engage in what Bakhtin calls an "absolutely free investigation of it." Imagine what might happen if educators took this conception of laughter seriously and made a point of using laughter to introduce new material, letting students inquire fully into the topic, turning it inside out and upside down, never fearing a question that cannot be easily answered, welcoming critique, debate, and multiple interpretations and perspectives.

Fear, Bakhtin asserts, is "the extreme expression of narrow-minded and stupid seriousness" (1984b, p. 47) but is defeated by laughter. He explains that laughter "frees human consciousness, thought, and imagination for new potentialities." He elaborates, "For this reason, great changes, even in the field of science, are always preceded by a certain carnival consciousness that prepares the way" (p. 49). Laughter permits us to destroy the official picture of events, forcing us to take a new look at them, to re-interpret them in the light of alternative possibilities. This is, in all likelihood, the great attraction of political cartoonists who make fun of those in power and their official and officious acts and pronouncements. In a more contemporary vein, this is the laughter prompted by the many blogs appearing daily in our email boxes or on alternative Web sites, blogs that offer unconventional, sometimes bitingly critical, sometimes excruciatingly funny perspectives and interpretations on the presumably authorized executive position.

Nothing escapes the laughter or parody of participants in carnival. Further, it must be noted that the laughter or parody of which Bakhtin spoke requires a certain level of knowledge. One cannot parody a political speech or act without considerable insight into its context, background, and the character of the players. In like fashion, one cannot satirize a speech, a prayer, or a sermon without first having studied and gained insight into its essence. In addition, one cannot develop a caricature of a public figure without having carefully observed her in daily life.

Instead of shutting down this type of laughter and parody in schools, educators might do well to encourage it. Having students develop parodies of historical characters, of current political decisions, of policy directions and so forth might well lead to a more enjoyable learning environment, but also to deeper understanding of the issues involved and insight into possible alternatives. We are quick to silence or discipline the class clown and when we do, we fail to acknowledge that the levity added to a situation could provide a brief moment of carnivalesque respite in the seriousness of a lesson intended to raise test scores and to promote the school as successful rather than failing.

The lesson to be learned from the role of carnivalesque laughter is not to take ourselves too seriously, not to become so focused on a test, a learning outcome, an objective to be covered, that we lose sight of the creative, the regenerative, the possible as a focus for learning.

The Role of Opposites

Bakhtin repeats his assertion throughout his discussion of the various attributes of carnival that their essence is transient. There is nothing fixed, absolute, or stagnant about carnival. Each time we engage in laughter, crowns a temporary ruler, puts on a mask, uses marketplace language, performs an eccentric or grotesque act, or forms a misalliance, we are freed from the constraints of everyday life to examine the world in new ways. Carnivalesque laughter, for example,

> Could grasp and comprehend a phenomenon in the process of change and transition, it could fix in a phenomenon both poles of its evolution in their uninterrupted and creative renewing changeability: in death birth is foreseen and in birth death, in victory defeat and in defeat victory, in crowning a decrowning. (1984a, p. 164)

Nevertheless, he says, even the foregoing is not an accurate depiction of what actually happens in carnival. If we state that something is "foreseen," it gives the impression that one thing logically flows into the other, that birth and death follow one another in a logical, predictable sequence, to some extent separate and distinct from one another. This is not really the impression Bakhtin wants to convey. He explains, "In living carnival images, death itself is pregnant and gives birth, and the mother's womb giving birth becomes a grave" (p. 164).

Bakhtin's world is a world of "both-and," and of irreconcilable tensions and paradoxes; it is a world of wholes:

> Death is not a negation of life seen as the great body of all the people but part of life as a whole— its indispensable component, the condition of its constant renewal and rejuvenation. Death is here always related to birth: the grave is related to the earth's life-giving womb. Birth-death, death-birth, such are the components of life itself. (1984b, p. 50)

Here, in the world of wholeness and continuation, we come to recognize that every aspect of life is a necessary part of the whole. No person, no idea, no event should be discounted.

For the educator, this message, although couched in new language, is likely not new. Seeing the potential in every child is, in fact, our mandate. Rejecting deficit thinking that considers early learning difficulties or socio-economic disadvantage as absolute, is essential. Everything we do as educators, whether we have realized it or not, implies this notion of regeneration and possibility, of wholeness and interconnection that is characteristic of Bakhtin's carnival.

The Potential of Carnival

For Bakhtin the promise of carnival is that it presents the possibilities in all their fullness. There are no dichotomies, no absolutes—only the ever-changing opportunities presented when one is freed from fear and constraint and able to live life joyfully. Bakhtin is not unrealistic. He understands that carnival is not and cannot be a permanent state. It is nevertheless a mechanism for creating wholeness. Carnival brings together Bakhtin's other key concepts: the notion of chronotope, of heteroglossic communication, and of living dialogically. He says that:

> Everything must be mutually reflected and mutually elucidated dialogically. Therefore all things that are distant and separated must be brought together in a single "point" in space and time. And for this the *freedom* of carnival and carnival's artistic conception of space and time are needed. (1973, p. 146)

This bringing together of things that are normally separated occurs because "this carnival sense of the world possesses a mighty-life-creating and transforming power, and indestructible vitality" (1984a, p. 107).

Carnival, Bakhtin argues, belongs fully to the people—all the people. The form which he admires, medieval carnival, occurred on the public square, on the adjacent streets, and to be sure also "invaded the home." Yet it is the concept of the square, representative of the fullness of public life that engages us still. There the drama of everyday life played out

in its wholeness—from the trial of a criminal, to the announcement of a new law, to a philosophical discussion about the meaning of citizenship—all were displayed for everyone to hear. Bakhtin writes in words and phrases we have heard before:

> Carnival knows neither stage nor footlights. But the central area could only be the square, for by its very idea carnival *belongs to the whole people,* it is *universal, everyone* must participate in its familiar contact. The public square was the symbol of communal performance . . . it could be said (with certain reservations, of course) that a person of the Middle Ages lived, as it were, *two lives:* one was the *official* life, monolithically serious and gloomy, subjugated to a strict hierarchical order, full of terror, dogmatism, reverence, and piety; the other was the *life of the carnival square,* free and unrestricted, full of ambivalent laughter . . . (1984a, pp. 128–129)

Carnival, as Bakhtin conceives of it, does not result in a person feeling more fragmented, pulled between the gay and glittering life of the carnival square and the dull, and stodgy routine of daily life. Instead, carnival pierces the routine. It brings everyone together in its routines of joyous participation and performance: there are no marginalized, subordinate, second-class citizens during carnival. Hence, it presents to all the possibility of a life that is less restricted, more communal, and more fully human.

If educators are to take seriously the potential of the previous three chapters for changing and improving the schooling experiences of children (and adults), we will also have to take seriously the concept of carnival, deciding how it might be introduced, creating the conditions under which it may arise and flourish.

At the same time, we acknowledge that carnival is not a strategy or a program. Too much planning or too tight orchestration will stifle it before it begins. We can and we must create some conditions under which carnival may occur. We can develop dispositions that welcome the spontaneous, the unexpected, the joyful and irreverent participation of all students, and the laughter that leads to intense

learning. Carnival, though, must not be introduced as a reform effort, with new policies, additional rules and guidelines; for to do so would destroy its fabric and essence. As educators we will need to set aside the temptation to codify carnival with rules and guidelines, to determine when it can or cannot be introduced, or to schedule it as a formal part of the school routine. Carnival must be spontaneous. We can create spaces and even times on the calendar when specific events that may promote a carnivalesque approach are likely to occur. But we cannot package, "implement," or evaluate carnival.

I recall a New Zealand educator describing what was obviously a time of carnival in her school. She reported that every year a huge water fight broke out some time during the spring—a fight in which students, teachers, and school administrators participated. Gradually, as the weather improved, and signs of spring became evident, one could see students bringing the largest water guns available and stashing them in their lockers. If one looked closely, one could also see teachers with their own water weapons carefully placed on the floors of their cars. At a point that no one could predict, someone simply initiated the fight and everyone participated for the next hour or two. Formal studies were suspended and everyone engaged in the activity, none worrying about who was getting wet, who was shooting whom, and so forth. This event, a temporary, anticipated, yet unscheduled annual activity at the school, she reported, was an excellent example of carnival as Bakhtin might have anticipated it.

In one sense, carnival is the culmination of Bakhtin's world view in that it is the mechanism which makes possible the rest. Carnival teaches us how to live fully in the chronotope of space/time introduced in Chapter 1. It reminds us of the importance of the utterance in heteroglossic communication and teaches us new ways of interacting in a new context: the bawdy, profane, parody, and familiar that we have been so carefully schooled to inhibit in public life. We have learned that when we live in

carnivalesque ways, we are living dialogically—open to difference, to other, to possibility.

In the next chapter, we shall attempt to put the ideas together and to imagine what education and educational leadership, informed by Bakhtin's innovative and appealing worldview, might actually be like.

GLOSSARY

Elitism—the belief that certain persons or members of certain classes or groups deserve favored treatment by virtue of their perceived superiority in such areas as intellect, social status, or financial resources. The sense of entitlement enjoyed by such a group or class often results in control, rule, or domination by that group or class.

Carnival—a way of breaking down hierachical barriers and power inequities.

Grotesque—refers to aspects of life about which we are often ashamed or embarrassed (bodily functions, ugliness, and death) but which are simply part of life and should not been seen as static, "hostile, alien, and inhuman." In Bakhtin's carnival, the grotesque often refers to a combination of natural forms and monstrous figures intertwined in bizarre or fanciful ways.

Mask—refers not only to physical masks but also to metaphorical ones—ways in which we hide our true selves from one another.

Parody—a way of imitating someone in a satirical or humorous way.

Schooling With a Difference

I stood on the sidewalk outside the front doors, trying to get a feel for the school and to understand
some of the dichotomies I knew to be true. I stared
at the rows of impressive new brick houses, the
empty field behind the school, and watched with
interest as several parents wearing saris or turbans
arrived to pick up their children. As I readied my
camera to take a picture of the school itself, I was aware
of a strangely dressed figure bounding out the front
door to greet me. I first focused on long red pointed
shoes at the end of slender, red legs; my gaze rose to
take in a short, elf-like tunic and a pointed jester
hat with flags attached to it. The slim, blond woman
with a red-painted face smiled—and only then did
I recognize her as the principal of the newly opened
Kororoti[1] Elementary School. With a grin, she reported
that this was a special day, in that the school had chosen to participate in a national walk to raise money
for cancer relief and everyone had agreed to wear
the school's colors: red and white. She quickly ush-
ered me into the gymnasium and invited me to

observe the children from many different ethnic and cultural groups sitting on the floor, eating and chatting quietly.

As I thought about carnival, dialogue, communication, and chronotope my thoughts kept returning to this scene and to the poster prominently displayed in the staff room. It showed a young girl, with a large sun bonnet and bare feet, happily perched in a tree, eating an apple and reading a book. Placed over the picture were the words: "At Kororoti we do things differently." What a great exemplar of education that reflects much of Bakhtin's worldview.

In this chapter, I want to begin by describing the approach to education introduced at Kororoti Elementary school, not primarily to hold the school up as a beacon or a light house, but in order to demonstrate that education that draws on and is reflective of Bakhtin's work is not only possible, but highly effectual even in a large North American public district and in a time of increased public pressure for performance and accountability. In this chapter, I take as a starting point, some of the ways in which Kororoti Elementary School has chosen to "do things differently." Then I expand the chapter to engage in some imagining of my own about what these choices might mean if the staff and educators in other organizations, including secondary schools, colleges, and universities, were to take some inspiration from Bakhtin's work.

Kororoti Elementary School

Kororoti opened in August 2005, with considerable fanfare (and some criticism) as the area's first balanced calendar (year-round) school. On opening day, the new three-storey brick building, designed to hold 1,000 children, was already full to capacity, had a waiting list of 100 children, and was using several portable "cottages" placed around the school-yard. When I visited six weeks after the opening, the principal was busily engaged in interviewing and hiring additional teachers. Behind the desk in principal Janice Harris's (also a pseudonym) office, is a carved wooden sign saying "dream"; and on the walls are various media clippings about the opening of the school—stories in Spanish, French, and Chinese as well as English. One full-page spread covered the school's first annual community barbecue and open house, an opportunity for parents and the wider community to meet the teachers and see the school. Pictures of the event show balloons, crowds of people, food, and a winding line of adults (the caption says "parents and teachers") and children holding hands, participating in the "dance"—all reminiscent of Bakhtin's carnival in which distinctions are removed, and everyone participates together. This event was the new school's creative version of a traditional "meet the teacher night," one which overcame most of the difficulties of encouraging attendance, and which successfully enticed parents from various cultural and socioeconomic backgrounds to participate.

Although it was the balanced calendar that received the most media coverage, it is not the only innovation at Kororoti School where the choice of the name was not incidental but central to the way in which learning, curriculum, and pedagogy are conceived. The astronaut herself, we are told in the first newsletter published by the school, is not only a "risk-taker," a woman who chose to go into space, but "continues to be a life-long learner"—a photographer, published author, neuroscientist, and a medical doctor. In fact, shortly after my visit to the school to make a formal presentation to the staff, I received a package in the mail. To my surprise, it contained two art posters, artistic photographs of nature by the astronaut Kororoti herself.

The décor of the school, while subtle, emphasizes the notion of space, exploration, and lifelong learning. The walls of each floor are painted in soft tones of brown, blue, and aquamarine to reflect the soil, air, and water of planet earth. The tiled floors are enhanced by random clusters of contrasting tiles, intended to represent galaxies—not those already discovered, but those which the children will name and explore. In order to encourage wide participa-

tion by parents and community members (both individuals and businesses) and to raise funds for additional sports and science equipment and other resources needed by a new school, the public is invited to purchase a star—small ones $25; medium $50, large $75, or extra large $100 or even a galaxy ($1,000 please)—to be painted on the dark blue ceiling of the front foyer. A time capsule in the form of a space shuttle is firmly attached to another blue wall in the foyer. Children are invited to take advantage of the "Chance to be a Shining Star" and to participate in one of several four-day intersession programs to be offered during the vacation periods (at a cost of $30 a day—less, we are told, than available day-care).[2] The first was related to ecological responsibility; the next to space exploration.

The approach to discipline is called "Reach" (respect, excellence, accountable, co-operation, harmony), with those achieving recognition being called "Stars." True to its theme, the school has various clubs with such names as "Peacemakers" or "Passionate Earthlings." The latter group not only had the opportunity to plant a number of shrubs and flowers donated by a local nursery, but the students also wrote definitions of the earth, one of which, published in the December 2005 newsletter included the following:

> Earth is . . . a home where you are living.
> Earth is . . . a present, what gift are you giving?
> Earth is . . . a track, you're running your race.
> Earth is . . . in darkness, in outer space.
> Earth is . . . delicate, as a petal of a rose.
> Earth is . . . a path, which way have you chosen?

Running through the poem, as through the activities themselves, one can see the emphasis on social responsibility, harmony, and respect that is characteristic of the whole school community.

Conceived of four years before by the district's "Creative Learning Choices Committee," the school's innovative package of scheduling and programs was approved as a three-year pilot project, one that would involve annual reports to both the board and the school council, but in which everyone recognized, as the program proposal stated, that "the success of the academic achievement of students must be considered on a longer-term basis" (Hamilton, 2005, p. 12). From the outset, it was apparent that, although the "Research and Evaluation Committee" of the district would support and assist with the evaluation of the pilot, the task would be shared by a committee of elected teachers, school administrators, district leaders, and an outside researcher. Teachers would not only be permitted, but encouraged, to develop their own action-research projects, and to work towards advanced degrees using the opportunity to investigate their own practices and the innovative approach of the school. Shortly after the school opened, a motivational and inspirational speaker from the district office informed the school staff that they were the PR team for the school; only the enthusiasm and communication skills of the whole staff would enable accurate and adequate dissemination of information about the project. An atmosphere of carnival, enthusiasm, and fun were so prevalent at the school that at the first meeting of the evaluation team, when the district superintendents walked into the meeting room, they were greeted by the chosen team of teachers and the principal and vice-principal wearing their red carnival hats. In the December 2005 newsletter, the student parliament's "prime minister" announced that they were sponsoring a food drive and wrote that if they reached their goal, "Mrs. Harris, our principal, will dress up as a toddler" and stated, "I'm sure there will be other staff members who will take on the challenge presented by their classes."

Despite the fact that all teachers are conscientious about the work of educating children, the theme of creativity and fun has been present from the outset. Principal Janice informed me that when she was interviewing teachers, she had given them five minutes to "impress her." Instead of the usual portfolios, many teachers demonstrated considerable initiative and creativity. One wrote a song which repeated her name in the chorus—a song Janice says

she still remembers. Another brought a number carpet and showed how she would use it to teach math—an approach she has now shared at staff meetings with the other primary teachers. Someone talked about a shoe; another showed pictures. Still another spoke poignantly about a child he had known in a previous school and the impact the child had made on him. Janice was not looking only for the outgoing, gregarious, and innovative, but for those who cared about and could develop relationships with the children, and as far as possible, for a balance of younger and more experienced teachers, male and female, and for ethnic diversity.

The need for the staff not only to be diverse, but to understand how to bring the diverse cultures of the students into the classroom is not only apparent when one visits the school and sees the diversity of the student body, but is evident in many of the school's initiatives. The September 2005 newsletter taught parents about special celebrations related to Sikh, Hindu, and Muslim cultures. An insert in the November newsletter informed parents about Diwali and Eid-ul-Fitr and invited them to permit their children (for a cost of 50 cents) to put on Mehndi/Henna. The newsletter explained that "the designs have no religious meaning, but are simply for decoration and beauty." It went on to describe the process of making the mehndi paste from henna leaves and stated that "when the paste is dried and washed off, an orange/red color will remain on the hands." The paste which is made of natural ingredients will absorb gradually into the skin within a period of one to two weeks.

It is not the single events or activities described here that are undertaken by the staff and students at Kororoti that are most striking, but the atmosphere of collaboration, dialogue, and fun which permeates the life of the school and which is immediately apparent to visitors whether they observe the classrooms, a staff meeting, activity in the gym or on the playground, or simply watch as children wait to be picked up or to board the buses at the end of the day.

The key themes explicated in the previous chapters are clearly evident here. There are regular efforts in large and small ways to live in chronotope—to connect the past of the children and their families with the present and future. Heteroglossia (multiple voices and perspectives) is the norm—with significant effort expended by all staff to acknowledge the importance of dialogue rather than monologue. Dialogue, as we have seen previously, is not simply talk, but an ontology—an approach to life in which one remains open to others and to outside and often unfamiliar concepts and perspectives. Dialogism undergirds the interactions among staff, between staff and students, students and students, and staff and parents. Furthermore, as indicated above, a carnivalesque spirit pervades every aspect of school life to such an extent that, when school closed for the Christmas vacation, instead of rushing to their cars to return home for the vacation, staff formed a long chain and danced around the school, through the halls, up and down stairs, picking up teachers still in their classrooms, joining in songs of joy and celebration, winding and singing for over half an hour.

A Novel Approach to Schooling: Putting It Together

It is not my intent in the foregoing description of some aspects of the life and organization of Kororoti Elementary School to suggest that this is *the* way to implement what one might call a Bakhtinian approach to schooling or educational leadership. Instead, I hope it has piqued your curiosity and helped you to begin to reflect on ways in which *your* organization might be renewed using some of the concepts we have discussed. In this section of the chapter, I want to take a more systematic approach to thinking about what might be different in our educational institutions and our approaches to the task of schooling both children and adults if we began to take seriously the novel approaches implied by Bakhtin's work.

Table 5.1 contains, on the left side, a number of words suggestive of the ways in which we typically

and traditionally (either implicitly or explicitly) think about and organize formal education. Yet, if these concepts are dominant, we could agree, especially after this careful consideration of Bakhtin's work, that this approach to schooling is too narrow and limited. Much as a boa constrictor squeezes the life out of its victim, the ways in which we too often conceptualize education result in institutions of learning that are lifeless rather than exciting and vital places of learning. This is not to say there is nothing worthwhile in current approaches to education because, of course, there is. It is not to suggest that everything we currently do is wrong, or bad, or evil. Instead, the list on the right is intended to offer alternative and additional ways of thinking about education, to provide new and novel ways of thinking that might make our approach to education more complete, more vital, even more "successful," although I recognize the dangers of using such a contested term.

Table 5.1. A Bakhtinian approach to education

Traditional Schooling	Bakhtin's "Novel" Approach
Promotes disengagement	Emphasizes agency
Focuses on mastery	Encourages inquiry
Confined by "habitus"	Embraces outsidedness
Remains static and boring	Increases vitality
Is monologic	Demands dialogism
Requires certainty & absolutes	Requires ambiguity
Requires completion	Accepts incompleteness
Fragments knowledge	Contextualizes learning
Is primarily receptive	Is active & reflective
Focuses on simple explanations	Acknowledges complexity
Remains fixed and closed	Is open
Is hierarchical	Is relational
Fears diversity	Assumes diversity

Many of the words on the list, as many of Bakhtin's concepts, flow into one another, making discrete discussion difficult. At the same time, there are enough subtle differences among these concepts so critical to more complete and liberating ways of thinking about education that I will address them separately. The two lists do not constitute opposites; they are not binaries—for to consider them in that fashion would be to misunderstand and distort the fundamentals of Bakhtin's thinking. At the same time, if we limit our educational approaches, practices, or policies to concepts similar to those on the left, we are actually constricting the potential and possibilities of our educational organizations. To constrict something is to make it smaller; to squeeze, or cramp, or compress it, restricting its scope or freedom. This is, to be sure, not the image we want of education—an institution intended, I would argue, to offer the opposite—to widen our horizons, to deepen our understanding, to expand our store of information, and to liberate our hearts, minds, and souls. Indeed, if we take seriously the Bakhtinian ideas explicated here, and introduce them into our ways of thinking about schooling, this is exactly what may happen.

Emphasizing Agency

We began our examination of Bakhtin's work with his concept of chronotope—a notion of time and space that opposed biographical time to adventure time. Bakhtin was clear that in adventure time we live through a series of chance occurrences, believing we have, and can have, no control over any of the events of our lives. Sometimes, as we have seen, educators seem to believe they are powerless. They talk as though they can have no impact because too many of the children in their classes have special needs, come from homes where English is not spoken fluently, or live in situations of poverty or abuse.

Educators must of course live in biographical time, not adventure time. However, this does not mean that we need to be engaged in every cause that comes our way or that we can take on every

social ill in order to be effective. It does require that we live agentically, that we acknowledge we have agency and can make a difference. Ogawa (2005) explains that "agency involves the control that people exert over their destiny, which is matched against deterministic forces assumed to lie largely beyond their control" (p. 90). As educators, it is important to acknowledge that while some things may well lie outside our control (such as the mandates of the U.S. No Child Left Behind legislation), many decisions and choices are ours to make.

The work of Nancy Fraser may be useful here. She distinguishes among various situations which educators might wish to address, especially when dealing with inequity, and asserts that different strategies are needed to address inequities that systematically disadvantage some groups of people vis-à-vis others. She proposes

> to distinguish two broadly conceived, analytically distinct understandings of injustice. The first is socioeconomic injustice, which is rooted in the political-economic structure of society . . . The second kind of injustice is cultural or symbolic and is rooted in social patterns of representation, interpretation, and communication. (1995, pp. 70–71)

For the first, socioeconomic inequity, she posits that a form of redistribution is called for to redress economic injustice. However, when the inequities are inherently social or cultural, she calls for some sort of cultural or symbolic change. Both types of change require a two-pronged approach involving one or both of affirmation and transformation. She explains:

> By affirmative remedies for injustice I mean remedies aimed at correcting inequitable outcomes of social arrangements without disturbing the underlying framework that generates them. By transformative remedies, in contrast, I mean remedies aimed at correcting inequitable outcomes precisely by restructuring the underlying generative framework. (p. 82)

Educational leaders can exercise their power to make a difference to the learning climate within the school, perhaps by instituting new programs such as one for "teen parents" involving academic support and child care. This does not directly transform the social conditions that sometimes contribute to teen parenthood or make it difficult for parents to continue with their education, but at the same time, may permit young parents to be both better educated and better equipped to address the needs of their children. Over time, this may have a transformative function as well. Although many educators are disposed to engage in what is sometimes known as "social action" or "activism," it is also important to note that the second prong, social transformation, does not always need to be taken up directly by educators in order for us to effect change.

In similar fashion, there may be a time and place for students to be "disengaged." They cannot be formally engaged in active learning at every moment of the day. In part for that reason, schools implement schedules that include time for play and relaxation (recess, breaks between classes, free periods, gym classes, and so forth). Disengagement, though, cannot be the norm, either for students or educators if schools are to accomplish their purposes related to learning.

Agency, therefore, requires active engagement in learning. It requires that educators will take responsibility for ensuring that all students are learning, but it also assumes that they will turn some of the decision-making and control over to students who must also be actively involved in their own learning. It is not enough for teachers to take active control, but then insist that students sit passively, listening and taking notes, never becoming actively or fully engaged in sense-making activities which constitute meaningful learning.

Madeleine Grumet (1995) has defined curriculum as "the conversation that makes sense of things." She explains, "It is the process of making sense with a group of people of the systems that shape and organize the world that we can think about together" (p. 19). A science assignment might, for example, require students to read the electric meter on the

side of their house for a period of two weeks and then come back to school and report their explanation for the highest and lowest periods of energy use. This assignment would, in many ways, be considered one that requires active learning. However, when several students come back to class, indicating they could not complete the assignment, teacher agency will take over, as the teacher explores the reasons for the students' failure to complete the assignment. If, on further investigation, she finds the students were simply disinterested, then one course of action may be required. On the other hand, should she determine that a student lived in a low-income subsidized high-rise apartment without individual meters and was too embarrassed to say so, she might take a different course of action. Here she will need to understand that the student may have felt excluded and disenfranchised not only by that particular assignment, but day after day, week after week, and year after year, and has come to the point of believing that school is not for him, that no matter how he attempts to exercise agency, he cannot succeed. New ways of thinking about, offering alternatives to, and completing the assignment must be found.

Disengagement may be a temporary state that offers relief from intense involvement, but when it becomes the normal or dominant way of thinking about the ability of either students or teachers to perform their task, then it constricts the possibilities of schooling. The key is that we are agentic human beings and must live in that fashion, in the fullness of chronotope time. We cannot blame others for our success or failure, but we must take responsibility to teach, to learn, and to make a difference.

Encouraging Inquiry

Just as there might be some place for disengagement, there may well be a time and a place for what is commonly known by educators as "mastery." At the same time, if we take Bakhtin's notions of incompleteness seriously, we will acknowledge that mastery may only be a stepping stone to more meaningful learning. A student may need to "master" some basic math facts (or at least the use of a calculator to attain them), but this cannot be considered mastery of mathematics. Instead, the student must be encouraged, as many approaches to the teaching of mathematics now do, to identify alternative ways of understanding and solving problems, and to determine which approach is right for him or her.

Although it may be necessary to know the main characters of Shakespeare's *Hamlet* and to be able to describe the relationship between his uncle and mother that may have contributed to Hamlet's despair, such is not the kind of mastery implied by Bakhtinian notions of outsidedness or dialogue. To engage in sense making conversations and come to one's own conclusion (which can then be shared and debated with others) about the rightness or wrongness of suicide, constitutes a different type of mastery learning—and one which unfortunately is rarely valued as highly in a culture in which learning is primarily assessed by right answers on standardized tests. There may well be no conclusive answer about suicide that holds for all students, from all backgrounds, and all cultures—but here, what may be of particular importance are the reasoning processes and the values identified during the sense-making conversations.

Inquiry is open-ended, inconclusive, unfinished in that we can never know everything, read every book on a topic, hear every perspective on a historical event, and so forth. When schools are organized only around mastery, they deny students the opportunity to develop the dispositions that lead to openness and inquiry sometimes referred to as lifelong learning. Perhaps even more importantly, they deny a student the opportunity to understand that his perspective is not the only perspective, that her approach is not the only approach, or that his interpretation can be enhanced, challenged, modified, and extended if he listens carefully to the thinking of others.

Embracing Outsidedness

Bourdieu's (1990) *habitus* is a useful concept that helps us understand why things are the way they are, why certain dispositions have become, over time, so enduring, and why people appear so attached to particular ways of acting and entrenched in particular modes of thinking. Teachers approach their educative tasks at their peril if they do not take time to understand the traditions and the social, cultural, and political norms of their workplaces. An educator trained in a Western, English-speaking country might, for example, go into a classroom in China (or for that matter, into a classroom of recent Chinese immigrants in North America), teach a lesson, and then ask, "Are there any questions?" Hearing none, the teacher might believe students had completely understood the concepts and task at hand and move on, either to teach the next topic or step, to assign some homework, or to administer a unit test. The teacher might then express amazement when she finds that only 10% of the students passed the test, and complain about their apathy and lack of agency, given that none asked any questions when given the opportunity. If told that in China it is considered rude of students to ask questions because it implies that the teacher did not do a thorough and adequate job of explaining the lesson, the teacher might take a different approach and would certainly understand the lack of questioning in a new light.

It is, therefore, important to understand norms and traditions, but not to be confined or constrained by them. When presented with the opportunity to organize reading groups by competency instead of by age and grade, many teachers resist, believing the temporary reorganization might damage some children's self-esteem. When provided the opportunity to institute a balanced calendar school year to redistribute some of the long summer vacation to holidays throughout the year and hence to reduce some of the summer learning loss, particularly of students from socioeconomically disadvantaged homes, many parents and educators resist. One typical response is that the current year was "good enough for us, so it should be good enough for our children." When an exchange teacher from New Zealand suggests to North American teachers that it is possible to stagger school entry and to permit children to enter kindergarten on their fifth birthday rather than to have all students in the class begin on the same day, most North American teachers respond with incredulity and wonder how one could possibly handle the chaos. Each of these ideas comes from the "outside." Each is in fact, an idea that has been relatively widely implemented in some areas and with considerable success. However, if we remain within our *habitus,* resisting new ideas because they are unfamiliar to us, we lose the possibility of expanding rather than constricting our options. We also lose the possibility of finding alternatives that might better meet the learning needs of at least some of our students.

Increasing Vitality

An American teacher once commented to me that February is "the time of year when teachers are tired of reiterating expectations and students are tired of hearing them." She went on to tell me that educators are "feeling taxed with the demands of our profession" and perhaps with the continual drive for accountability. In such cases, schools tend to lose their vitality. When teachers are stressed, students tend to respond with some degree of lethargy and disinterest. If educators do not convey a sense of relevance and importance, even excitement about what they are teaching, students quickly come to believe the matter is inconsequential and unimportant.

It is at this point that a school might benefit from an injection of carnival. A winter carnival in which teachers and students compete together on the hockey rink or the soccer field can change the ways in which they relate to each other just enough for a new attitude to take hold in the classroom. One rarely sees such competition involving staff and students conducted in a lackluster and unenthusiastic way.

Instead, there is great excitement, teasing, jostling, good-natured name-calling, and a level of competition that generally far exceeds the stakes of the competition itself. The new ways of interacting, including the ability to tease or criticize one from whom one is normally separated by considerable distance of age, expertise, and authority seems to produce new energy and new enthusiasm. Turning the learning activity from quiet seatwork to a game may produce a similar response; as might changing the classroom norms and giving the students the opportunity to design the lesson or to complete a report using video rather than a print medium.

On one occasion, when I had to teach a difficult concept (Weber's theories of bureaucracy) to a group of educators embarking on a graduate program, I racked my brain for a way to bring the concepts alive. As I reflected, I recalled that a recently retired colleague who had previously taught the course was a thespian at heart, and so I phoned to ask him if he would be willing to attend class in the persona of Weber. At first, he refused; we chatted and hung up. After a few minutes, my phone rang and my colleague, intrigued at the thought of a somewhat carnivalesque moment and the opportunity to play a central role in it, accepted the invitation. His appearance exceeded my anticipation. He came, dressed in a long black cloak, a wig, leaning on a cane, pointing and gesticulating with a gnarled finger as he explained how most theorists had misinterpreted him and urged the class to understand his true intent. Although I had not intentionally introduced carnival into the classroom, that was the outcome. Moreover, it was so successful and so widely discussed, that subsequent years of students eagerly awaited Weber's annual appearance.

Vitality is not only a necessary part of pedagogy, but plays a role in every aspect of institutional life. If we are static, either in our attitudes, our organization, our procedures, or our structures, there is little anticipation, little excitement, as everything has become common and routine. In physics the concept of inertia refers to the tendency of a body to resist acceleration and to remain at rest. In social institutions, the concept has taken on slightly more pejorative undertones, and often implies not only a disinclination to change, but a disinclination to act at all. If we are to maintain the ability of our educational institutions to respond and react in ways that meet the needs, not only of our changing times and in ways that keep us closely connected to the past, but living in a new and dynamically different present (chronotope), we must maintain the vitality of our institutional life. Carnival is one way of accomplishing this.

Demanding Dialogism

Another important way in which we maintain institutional vitality is to ensure that the dominant mode of interaction within our institutions is dialogic rather than monologic. Monologism is a way of talking to ourselves, of perpetuating a certain way of thinking or a certain set of attitudes that are never questioned and never changed. When we take a monologic approach, there is only one person involved, one who is fixed in her ways and unwilling or unable to change. Everything else is irrelevant. Nothing can be learned from a book, a piece of music, a work of art, or another human being. In fact, Bakhtin suggests that monologism is akin to death. His attitude, as we saw earlier, is that "We must renounce our old monological habits in order to become comfortable" in an incomparably more complex world (1973, p. 229). In case we were in any doubt about our need for others outside ourselves in order to live and to grow, he explained that "a single voice ends nothing and resolves nothing. Two voices is the minimum for life" (1984a, p. 252).

For Bakhtin, we cannot truly live unless we are willing to accept and listen to the polyphony of voices, the heteroglossia of which humanity is composed. Because there are so many different ways of thinking, so many different norms and values, beliefs and attitudes, strengths and weaknesses, needs and

opportunities, it behooves the educator to reject the notion of "best practice" or the "one best way," and to develop richly nuanced repertoires of approaches for any task demanded of a school. Whether we are trying to build a sense of community, develop new extracurricular programs, institute a new reading series, or develop new policies with respect to linguistic attainment, we must not fall into the trap of thinking monologically.

Another useful way of thinking about this may be to consider the differences between what Cummins (1989) calls additive or subtractive approaches to educating children from non-dominant home backgrounds and languages. Too often, he suggests, educators develop approaches to instructing children from minority cultures in ways that disempower rather than empower them. We develop language programs that require them to forget (through lack of valuing and disuse) their primary languages. We exclude their parents and communities from participation in the decision-making processes of schooling. We provide **transmission-oriented pedagogy** which denies children the opportunity to bring their lived experiences into the classroom as a basis for sense-making conversations. Finally, Cummins suggests, we legitimize rather than assess. In other words, we use the test as a basis for showing how well we have taught something, rather than for assessing what students know and what they still need to learn. If students do not achieve the desired outcomes, we then locate "the 'problem' within the minority student" (p. 61) rather than in an examination of our pedagogy. These practices, Cummins explains, screen:

> from critical scrutiny the subtractive nature of the school program, the exclusionary orientation of teachers towards minority communities, and transmission models of teaching that inhibits students from active participation in learning. (p. 61)

If our education systems and practices remain closed to critical scrutiny, Cummins argues, we will continue to engage in practices that disadvantage minority children by disempowering them and their

Transmission-oriented pedagogy

refers to a form of instruction that considers it the teacher's task to transmit information seen as fixed and factual

families. When we deny students the ability to use their home languages and cultures, forcing them instead to adopt only the traditions of the dominant culture, when we engage in the other disempowering practices he described, excluding their parents and families from decision-making structures, telling rather than teaching, and legitimizing rather than assessing, we are engaged in subtractive practices that take away the children's and families' sense of identity, of confidence, and of self-worth. If we adopted practices that did not deny what children from "minority" and **minoritized** families already know, education could become empowering rather than disempowering and subtractive.

When we take a monologic approach to education, these limiting practices may occur. If, on the other hand, our approach is truly dialogic, we will not make decisions without including the voices of parents and community members; we will not make decisions that devalue or reject the learning students have already acquired; and we will not engage in assessment by assigning more value to predetermined answers than to the thinking and sense-making in which students engage.

Today's schools in many countries are more diverse than ever before. To successfully address this diversity, educators must engage with alternative perspectives, acknowledge the importance of listening to alternate voices, and ensure that we educators are engaged in the listening. If we see our role as telling, we have once again become monologic, and the minority parent or student becomes irrelevant. When we listen, as Delpit (1990) says, not only with "open eyes and ears, but open hearts and minds" (p. 101), we become dialogic.

It bears repeating, however, that dialogism bears nothing in common with either relativism or dogmatism. We saw previously that Bakhtin had addressed this very question directly, saying:

> It is hardly necessary to mention that the polyphonic approach has nothing in common with relativism (nor with dogmatism). It should be noted that both relativism and dogmatism equally exclude

Minoritized

refers to the marginalization and subordination of a group that expresses ideas, beliefs, or behaviors that contradict dominant norms. Minoritized groups are not necessarily the numerical minority.

all argumentation and all genuine dialog, either
by making them unnecessary (relativism) or impossible (dogmatism). (1973, p. 56)

As mentioned in Chapter 2, in the first few months
of 2006, a worldwide furor of sorts was spurred by
the earlier publication in a Danish newspaper of cartoons portraying the prophet Mohammed. Papers
in some other countries reprinted the cartoons in
the name of "freedom of the press," while in other
places, riots and protests (sometimes violent) broke
out. What struck me about the situation was how
many people decried the riots and/or criticized the
papers, but how little meaningful dialogue there
was. Moreover, most people stood back, watching,
as if to say, "Who am I to take a stand?" Locally,
two college newspaper editors were suspended because
they had "made the decision to publish some cartoons,
without full consultation with the other editors."
To me, this was a spurious argument. It permitted a
focus on process without any discussion of the merits of either publishing or withholding the cartoons;
it avoided an outcry without any need for a meeting of alternative perspectives, for listening to voices
from outside; and most importantly, it steered clear
of the need to take a position.

Bakhtin's notion of dialogue and dialogism was
not upheld. There was no examination of chronotope (space and time) and the history of either Islam
or of a free press. There was no discussion of nature
and history of cartooning and the non-iconic nature
of Muslim. There was no discussion of what sacred
means and hence no understanding of the possibility of sacrilege. Moreover, there was total silence
about the need to accompany rights with responsibility. In short, people seemed to take solace in their
solitary monologic position, preferring to be safe
than to interact with those who might have a different position. Dialogism does not permit this kind of
retreat to occur in our schools but urges the creation
of spaces (as Palmer has done) in which this kind of
exploration might take place in safety and a climate
of respect.

For many educators, this is a difficult suggestion. However, a Bakhtinian approach emphasizes that instead of being constrained by the necessity of dialogue, it is monologism that constrains and constricts us. Being open to others not only provides life-giving interaction and new ideas, but opens us to a new sense of freedom. Too often educators exhibit what Senge (1990) calls a learning disability, one which he identifies as the syndrome of "the enemy is out there" (p. 19) in which we fail to take responsibility for our actions, preferring instead to blame an unknown "they" as in "they won't let me. . . ." Acknowledging the agency we have, listening carefully to alternative voices and perspectives, and carefully considering new ideas can lead to a kind of freedom that many educators never seem to experience in their work.

The lack of spontaneity and freedom are particularly curious given the reality that there are so few actual controls on what occurs behind a classroom door. There are, undoubtedly, sets of norms and expectations, goals and accountability measures, but overall the enterprise of education survives according to what Meyer and Rowan (1977) called the "logic of confidence." They maintained that the credibility and enforcement of the profession of education resides largely with the accreditation and certification processes which lead to becoming a teacher, but that once in the profession, there is little uniformity and little formal pressure to conform. If one doubts this analysis, one generally has to look no further than the variation among teacher-made tests within a single school for students taking the same course and learning the same concepts.

This awareness is important because sometimes educators believe we are less free than we are. We certainly often act as though there were shackles constraining our pedagogical activities. The typical response that we must "cover the content," for example, is one of perceived constraint. However, educators are rarely assessed on the extent to which we have had students turn every page, complete every exer-

cise, or discuss every topic; instead the measure of a good teacher frequently seems to be determined by how well students do on tests. Thus, being accountable for students' test results is not the same as being held to "covering the content" in traditional linear, sequential, and too often fragmented and transmissive ways but allows for creative and innovative ways to help students learn new concepts.

Moreover, having students do well on tests, although of real importance in today's era of accountability, is not and should not be the only measure of excellence in education. Preparing students for participation in civic life and teaching the dispositions and attitudes which will permit them to live dialogically in diverse and heterogeneous communities are also of utmost importance despite the lack of formal measurement of some of these most important attributes.

As educators, if we live clearly in chronotope time space, take seriously the plurality of the voices that comprise a school, and learn to live dialogically, we will find a sense of freedom that we may never have anticipated.

Achieving an Ambiguous Unity

It may seem particularly convoluted to assert that the more we feel the need to be certain, the less unity we may feel, and the more fragmented our approach to life may seem. Paradoxically the more we embrace ambiguity, the more at peace we may be, and the less fragmented and stressed we may feel, and the higher the quality of our moral life may be. At issue here is the need to understand that, as Bakhtin states, we need to live, fully aware of our status as "one who is evolving and developing, a person who learns from life" (1981a, p. 10).

The problem is that the more we strive for certainty, the more stress we impose on ourselves and on others, because there are few if any areas where there can be absolute certainty. Moreover, we saw in Chapter 3 how much easier it is to acknowledge that a "fully consistent message simply does not capture the complexity of moral life" (Sidorkin, 2000, p. 156) and to permit ourselves to engage in an inner moral dialogue than to resist new understandings, believing somehow that if we change our minds, we are guilty of moral weakness.

Parker Palmer (1998) emphasized that "good teaching cannot be reduced to technique; good teaching comes from the identity and integrity of the teacher" (p. 10). He explained that *"to teach is to create a space in which the community of truth is practiced"* (p. 90); and then he defined this community as one informed by constant inquiry and continuous dialogue. For Bakhtin, as well as for Sidorkin, Palmer, and others, the key is not to put pressure on ourselves to take an immutable position and maintain it all our lives, but to exercise our freedom to reflect, to encounter, to learn and grow in relationship with others. Helping students to live a moral and ethical life is one goal of education in most countries. Helping students to understand that this does not mean taking absolute positions which cannot be changed either by our own internal dialogue or by others is an extremely difficult but important task. When we assert, as educators, absolute moral values, we are, once again, being constricted by our own location and failing to remain open to the possibility that we are wrong.

Once again, this does not mean that we should not take a stand or act. We must. Further it is important for us to help students to do the same, not out of immutable certainty, but always listening to the inner voice that causes us to revisit our beliefs and actions in the hope of refining or extending them. An example may be useful here. Many educational leaders struggle with the need to hire educators who come from under-represented groups. At one point in my career, our university president came to visit our department to address the topic of diversity. Wanting to demonstrate how diverse our department already was, and the attention we had paid to the topic, I assembled some members of the department who would introduce themselves to her dur-

ing her visit. One was a Chinese woman, educated in France. Another was a Palestinian man who had recently moved from an Israeli university; another was a graduate student who had entered the country as a refugee and had often spoken eloquently about his struggles as an ethnic minority student. When the time came for everyone to speak, my student did not focus, as previously discussed, on his ethnically diverse background, but on his dual identity as a student and a teacher. I pressed him, wanting to make the previously agreed-upon point and in doing so, I failed to listen. I failed to respect his right to reveal himself as he had chosen. For the moment, my unwavering desire to represent us as "diverse," led me to a point of denying and disrespecting a friend and colleague. In that instant, my construction of diversity in terms of ethnic origin did not allow him to define and redefine diversity in other ways.

Accepting Incompleteness

Related to the notion of moral ambiguity is the need for educators to reject the absolutism that suggests there is only one way to interpret a fact or event, that argues that there are only certain books that constitute an acceptable "canon" for students to read, or that asserts there is no chance we might be wrong. Bakhtin stated that

> There is never a first nor a last word and there are no limits to the dialogic context . . . Even *past* meanings, that is, those born in the dialogue of past centuries, can never be stable (finalized, ended once and for all)—they will always change (be renewed) in the process of subsequent, future development of the dialogue. (1986e, p. 170)

These are sometimes difficult lessons to learn, given our upbringing in which parents and society as a whole often teach children in black and white terms. However, educators should not fall into this trap. Clearly much of what we were taught as students has been either disproven or at least challenged in many ways. For example, many North Americans

have been taught that Native Americans lived in primitive hunter-gatherer societies without systems of governance or law and hence unable to participate in civil society without being under "trusteeship." Sometimes, as a Canadian, I am forced to respond to questions from well-meaning tourists who ask if all Eskimos still live in igloos—an image carried over from outdated textbooks and stories from primary school. We continue to believe that Africans live in huts, that the Maori are bellicose, and so forth, despite the fact that these generalizations were never valid and are certainly misleading today.

We can never teach as though we were providing the last word on a subject, although, once again, this does not prevent us from providing current "state of the art" understandings. At one time, of course, people who dared to advance the theory that the earth rotated around the sun were shunned and punished as heretics. Once, it was believed that performing surgery on the human heart went against God's will. Previous medical science believed that the only treatment for tuberculosis was the separation from family and relocation of a patient to a sanitarium, while today's treatment is quite different. Once we passed laws requiring indigenous children to give up their native language and to only speak the language of the colonizer; today frantic efforts are underway in many countries to prevent these same native languages from becoming extinct.

Knowledge changes; values and perspectives change; and so too must our teaching. Moreover, it is important to teach this notion of **dynamic learning** to our students so they will not encounter dissonance and distress when new ideas supplant the old ones.

I am not talking about schooling in which there are no rules, no rights or wrongs, but I am suggesting we must leave room for development—social, intellectual, moral, and spiritual if we are to fulfill the promise of education. Education comes, after all, from the Latin word *educare* (to draw forth, "bring out," from *ex*- "out" + *ducere* "to lead"). It is our job

Dynamic learning
implies that what is learned and accepted as "truth" or "fact" at one time may change as new knowledge is acquired

to draw forth new ideas and old, to help students make connections between past and present and to look into the future. It is our task to draw out multiple voices, multiple perspectives, multiple ways of approaching and understanding the topics at hand.

Again, this is not to imply there can be no expectations—either for learning or for behavior. I recall the story told to me by a high school principal concerned about an interaction he had had with a student and an angry older male sibling. The student, who had recently arrived from India, had been involved in what the family considered to be an inappropriate friendship with a male student in the same school. Because the girl's father had returned to India on business, the older sibling was the "man of the house," left in charge of the family. To protect the honor of his family, he attempted to enter the school and to forcefully and violently defend his family's honor by beating up the offending male student. The principal was concerned that disciplining the boys for violent behavior was disrespectful to their traditions and family values. Here, it seems to me, is a clear cut illustration of the need for some certainty. Schools must be safe places for all students; they must be places where students are taught tolerance, respect, and perhaps even restraint. It is not permissible to exercise physical violence on another student in school. That said, it is important, though, as Bakhtin urged, to listen to and attempt to understand as fully as possible the other's position and then to determine together alternate, acceptable courses of action.

Bakhtin talked about authoritative voices that seem to be making pronouncements as if from on high—pronouncements that leave no room for contextual variation, and which provide no opportunity for individual discretion. Palmer urges us to take seriously the paradoxes on which life and education reside. He writes that the pedagogical space which works best for him is one "shaped by a series of paradoxes" (p. 73). This requires a space which is both bounded and open, hospitable and "charged,"

that invites the voice of the individual and the voice of the group, that honors the "little" stories of the students and the "big" stories of the disciplines and tradition, one which supports solitude and surrounds it with the resources of the community and that welcomes both silence and speech (p. 74). There are boundaries, but nothing unequivocally fixed in learning spaces in which multiple voices and perspectives are always present.[3]

Contextualized Learning

One educational implication of Bakhtin's chronotope is the importance of context, a point about which educators are increasingly aware. Even so, in today's climate of high stakes accountability, despite our knowledge that children, schools, and communities differ dramatically from one context to another (not to speak of intra- and international differences), there is a strong countervailing trend to move to standardize curricular and pedagogical practices. In some schools and districts, there is such a desire for standardization that teachers are asked to teach a particular lesson in a particular way on a specific day. Here one need not ask what the definition of education is and how standardization advances the cause because the constrictive nature of such an approach is abundantly clear.

As we saw earlier, Bakhtin urges the opposite. He explains that

> authoritative discourse permits no play with the context framing it, no play with creative stylizing variants on it. It enters our verbal consciousness as a compact and indivisible mass, one must either totally affirm it, or totally reject it. (1981d, pp. 342–343)

The salience of the need for contextualized learning may be quickly evident as we examine a few social trends from our own culture and then think about trends in teaching and learning as well. At one time, it was deemed inappropriate for women in North America to swim in a public place without wearing suits that provided considerable body

cover. Now, the practice is archaic. However, we seem to forget that North American traditions of modesty have changed when we decry out of hand the burqa worn in other countries as oppressive and disrespectful to women. The point is that cultures, norms, and values change and that it is more appropriate in a learning context to understand different trends and perspectives from various times and places than to attempt to impose one set of norms as right for all people in all contexts. Attempting to do so is not only undesirable and often disrespectful, but generally impossible.

Numerous less dramatic examples may be found on a daily basis in most schools. A central authority may tell teachers to use a specific approach (whole language or phonics, for example) to teach all children; we assign every child in a class the same homework with the same number of problems, regardless of their level of understanding and competence; we insist on "mainstreaming" all children to prevent elitism, without thinking about the real differentiated learning needs of different students. We assume that a bilingual program suitable for a Hispanic context (in which there has been a long written history and in which multiple texts are available) is suitable for a Navajo context in which neither parents nor children have grown up reading, writing, and speaking Navajo, and for which quite a different approach would be more desirable. The list is endless. As Bakhtin (among many others) reminds us: context matters.

Becoming Reflective, Acknowledging Complexity

If there is nothing fixed or finished, if everything is contextual or perspectival, then it becomes important to consider our pedagogical emphases once again. We will likely need to discover a new balance between transmitting information and providing spaces for students to engage in sense-making conversations and activities, encouraging them to reflect on what they know and to ask fundamental questions such as "whose perspective is being represented in this interpretation and whose might be different." Such an approach to teaching and learning is quite different from what one finds in most schools today.

In 1979, scholars Schwartz and Ogilvy conducted some research into ways in which various disciplinary thinking had changed and found that in every area they studied (philosophy, physics, religion and spirituality, mathematics, linguistics, the arts, brain theory, psychology, and more), there had been a basic shift in thinking in three areas: ordering, knowing, and causing. In terms of ordering, they found that there had been a fundamental shift from understanding the world to be a giant mechanical clock to recognizing the unpredictability and complexity of the universe. Once again, this does not imply there is no order, but that we understand that within order, there are patterns that are chaotic and that within chaos there are orderly and predictable occurrences. Chaos theory, for example, demonstrates that, although we cannot predict where an individual atom will move next, there are always underlying patterns developed by the movement of atoms in general. Where we cannot predict how an individual student will respond to a given piece of literature, there are some general trends we might anticipate as educators.

When Schwartz and Ogilvy described shifts in knowing, they described how we have moved in almost every discipline from thinking about knowledge as fixed and finite to a recognition that knowledge is also constructed and depends in large part on individual and cultural interpretations. For example, if I mention Paris and am thinking about Paris, France, while your thoughts immediately turn to Paris, Tennessee—the town where you were born, we will have a very strange and difficult conversation. When I happen to mention to colleagues that I am planning to spend some time in China, anticipating some of the wonderful steamed vegetables and hand-made noodles I have come to enjoy, I am often taken up short with a warning to carry my

own peanut butter. I have a son who is with a diplomatic corps in Pakistan. Frequently when I share this information, my listener responds with, "Oh, how dangerous. Aren't you worried?" To this, I generally respond that he is doing what he enjoys and believes to be important. What we know and have experienced strongly influences how we receive and perceive new information.

When Schwartz and Ogilvy discussed shifts in how causation is formulated in various disciplines, they focused on a general shift from a notion of "cause and effect" to a worldview in which there is general recognition that there are very few direct and absolute cause and effect relationships. In science, simply lowering the temperature of water to 0° C, for example, does not necessarily mean the water will freeze, because of course other factors such as salinity and wind velocity must also be taken into account. What Schwartz and Ogilvy noted was a move from single to multiple perspectives, from single explanations to multiple ones. One can no longer approach the world as one would an instruction manual following detailed directions to complete a task. One can no longer approach complex issues in black and white terms, but must come to embrace the in-between grey area.

Indeed, there is very little in science or social science that one can simply assert without **contextualizing** the information first. Despite the fact that we know better, and that Bakhtin wrote at length about the importance of dialogue, of interpretation, of understanding that the word or even the utterance apart from both speaker and listener signify nothing, we somehow persist in thinking that if we *teach a topic*, our students will have understood it. We insist on *covering* the curriculum, failing to be cognizant of the need for sense-making rather than passive receptivity if students are to be fully engaged in learning.

Again, receptivity in certain contexts is critically important. We have seen how Bakhtin gives primacy in dialogue to the listener. However, this is not simply a passive, receptive listening. Here it is receptivity of concepts and ideas that form the basis

Contextualizing

taking account of context and recognizing that values and truths may be interpreted differently in different situations

for dialogue and for understanding; and it is this type of listening we must foster in our educational organizations.

Becoming Open

When we take the time in schools to foster active and engaged listening and dialogic interaction, when we acknowledge the relevance of context, and emphasize the importance of outsidedness, of polyphony, or heteroglossia, we have moved a considerable distance along the path to becoming more open and less constricted. I think, with a smile, of the story told by one of my Muslim students of going to his son's pre-school class shortly before Christmas to discuss the Muslim festival of *Khushiali Mubarak,* a time of recognition of the birth of their living spiritual leader. After his wife had taught the children a typical "hand and kiss" gesture and everyone had participated in making greeting cards and sharing samosas, one pre-schooler turned toward my friend and asked, "Who's he?"

The ensuing dialogue was fascinating. One child stated, "He's Santa Claus. This prompted another to ask, "If you're Santa, where is your beard?" When Satish responded, "I shaved," another child asked, "Why aren't you wearing your red suit?" After the laughter had subsided, a small resolute voice from the back of the circle shouted, "He's not Santa, he's a black man."

The openness of this dialogue is striking. No one told the children that Santa had nothing to do with *Khushiali Mubarak;* no one hushed the child for saying that a "black man" cannot be Santa or that it was not "polite" to talk about the color of anyone's skin; and no one corrected him for mentioning Satish's color and describing him as black. There was openness to explore and space within which the children were safe to make sense of the situation as they saw it. Who could have known that it would be skin color, not the lack of a flowing white beard, not the absence of a stuffed red suit that would convince a child that Satish was not "Santa"?

Contrast the previous story with a situation presented to me in a graduate class by another student, himself a dedicated educator and vice-principal. He described how he had been shopping with his four-year-old daughter on the weekend when she audibly and pointedly asked about a woman shopping nearby, "Why is that woman brown?" He told me he had quickly drawn his child aside, and informed her that it was impolite to talk about color, that she might make the woman feel "uncomfortable."

When we have a fixed view of the world, we tend to think in terms of right and wrong, good and bad, polite and impolite, and fail to permit open and honest inquiry. Why should a four year old not wonder about differences in skin color? Why would having brown skin make someone feel uncomfortable—except, of course, because of the ways in which white adults often are uncomfortable with difference and hence, marginalize and exclude it?

On the one hand, being open and teaching children that asking honest (but respectful) questions and inquiring about what they do not know or understand is the basis for overcoming racism and hegemony. On the other hand, when we hush children up, conveying the message that there is something wrong, even with noticing, let alone talking about, skin color, we convey once again a sense that everything simply is the way it is and should neither be explored nor challenged. Teaching children, for example, to be "color-blind," never to acknowledge or discuss color is not, as is commonly understood, a form of tolerance and acceptance. Instead, it is a hegemonic way of teaching that we (who are often white and in positions of power) do not have to understand how another person's color may position him or her differently. We have the luxury of not seeing color and of saying, "We are all the same" while someone who knows her color has prevented her from gaining entry into a particular club or from being hired for a position of authority can only remain silent, for to do otherwise in a "color-blind" society is unacceptable.

Being open requires acknowledging that what has always been accepted may be wrong. To explore that possibility, according to Bakhtin, requires living in dialogic relations.

Becoming Relational

In the above instance, the exchange with Satish was based on an understanding of the world, and of the pedagogical setting, as relational. In the second, the world was constructed as hierarchical, with an adult telling a child what she could or could not say. (Again I am not here suggesting parents abrogate their roles as parents, or teachers as teachers, but simply suggesting that rules need to be firmly embedded in dialogic relationships.)

By asserting that a single voice resolves nothing and that two people are necessary for life, Bakhtin clearly emphasizes the importance of relationships. He says that "a particular means of reality can only be understood in connection with the particular means of representing it" (1994, p. 179). Moreover, he states that "completely new relationships are established" (1981a, p. 12) when we recognize the polyglot nature of our existence.

Polyphony permits one to become sensitive to the "immense plurality of experiences" (Holquist, 1981, p. xx). It is the basic unit of communication in which two people talking to each other begin to come to terms with infinite diversity. "In this actively polyglot world," Bakhtin says, "completely new relationships are established between language and its object" (1981a, p. 12), but also between and among individuals. Indeed, the polyglot universe is basic to life in schools, which must therefore become more open than it often appears at present.

We have seen how Bakhtin advances the notion of carnival as one way to overcome hierarchy, to break out of the often oppressive confines of tradition and to find new, more egalitarian ways of interacting. For him, a "carnival sense of the world possesses a mighty life-creating and transforming power, an indestructible vitality" (1984a, p. 107).

Principal Janice Harris breaks out of the hierarchy of her role by dressing in strange clothes, by going out onto the playground with her students and jumping rope, and by dancing in conga-type lines with teachers and parents. Most importantly, as she does so, she is forging new relationships, entering into the world of the students, or teachers, or parents, getting to know them on their ground and breaking down the formal barriers between herself and others. Then, when she finds it necessary to remind parents of the rules, that they should not drop their children off in front of the school in the bus lane, for example, she draws on the good will established through the relationship and gently reminds them of the "kiss 'n ride" area west of the school.

"In the beginning is the relation," wrote Buber (1970, p. 69). He expressed clearly, although in different words, the Bakhtinian notion of understanding through relationships when he explained, "When we walk our way and encounter a man who comes toward us, walking his way, we know our way only and not his; for his comes to life for us only in the encounter" (p. 124). Unless we take time to engage in encounter (and carnival is only one way of doing so), we can never know more than our own way; we can never learn about or from another, and we cannot develop to be more fully human.

Hierarchical structures were developed to overcome chaos and unpredictability, and to surmount the evils of nepotism and capriciousness in organizational life. Hierarchical structures maintain distance, provide appropriate chains of command, and require formality rather than familiarity. They were established as ways of governance that maintain order and discipline, but were never intended as mechanisms or vehicles of learning. For that reason, educators who work in bureaucratic and hierarchical institutions must take care not to let the structures interfere with the creation of relationships that foster learning.

Assuming Diversity

The key to Bakhtin's approach to diversity in an educational institution is not to think of it as a challenge or a problem, not even to celebrate it—except insofar as one celebrates life itself, because diversity just is. If we are to live, dialogically rather than monologically, open rather than closed, to learn and grow rather than wither from authoritarian voices either from outside or within our heads and hearts, then we must acknowledge that diversity is the basis for life. For that reason, educators must learn to live joyfully and dialogically within the heteroglossia of life, accepting, welcoming, and affirming each child regardless of intellectual or physical ability, home language or ethnic background, sexual orientation or religious perspective. Within every school and classroom, we find students with a range of ages, maturity levels, personalities, and interests. Some are introverts; some extroverts. Some are clumsy, some graceful. All are part of the complex fabric of human existence.

Bakhtin, of course, explained that if an idea remains only "in one person's isolated individual consciousness" it degenerates and dies. An idea gives birth to new ideas, he claims, "only when it enters into genuine dialogical relationships with other, *foreign,* ideas" (1986a, p. 7). Associating only with those like us or grouping students in ways that produce excessive homogeneity prevents the birth and development of new ideas, new understandings. Moreover, Bakhtin speaks of the need, not only to interact on emotional and intellectual planes, but also to develop spiritually. For this, he asserted the necessity of having the "organized coexistence and interaction of spiritual diversity" (1973, p. 25).

In some ways, this begs the need to support public schools—at least for schooling that is heterogeneous enough that students encounter diverse perspectives. As always, there are no absolutes with Bakhtin and no black or white interpretations that can guide our decision making. Solutions are always contextual, and there is no one "best way" or single

"best practice" that helps us teach or reach all children.

One contentious response to the need for diverse practices is charter schools. Some of these schools attract children from specific religious groups; some from single ethnic backgrounds; and some focus on children's abilities and interests. There is no doubt that such schools appear to fulfill a need in society, but when they stratify and divide children, rather than uniting them in a diverse and robust school community, we have created conditions under which it is difficult to become comfortable with diversity. I am not suggesting that all children should be taught in the same space and in the same way at the same time. However, I would contend that to help children and future citizens understand how to relate to, understand, and live in a diverse society, it is important to provide opportunities for social interaction. Bakhtin argued, after all, for everything to be temporary; and it would be my dream that separate non-public schools would be a temporary response to the failure of public schools to adequately understand and accept diversity.

I am reminded of an interaction I had with a teacher from a very successful (in terms of student academic achievement) and very homogeneous elementary school. When I asked if, and in what ways, the school took account of diversity in its approach to curriculum and pedagogy, the response amazed me. She replied, "No, we don't address diversity at all; we don't need to; we only have one or two minority students in this school." Too often, I believe, educators see diversity only in terms of dress or skin color, ignoring the other very real kinds of diversity in our classrooms. Even if it were possible to state with any degree of accuracy that there is little or no diversity in a given school or classroom, it seems to me to beg the question: how can we teach our children to live respectfully and with understanding in an increasingly mobile and diverse global community if we do not prepare them at school? Perhaps more importantly, how can we expect them to enjoy the freedom to learn and grow in meaningful ways i

we do not teach them the importance of dialogic relations with others?

There is one other point that should be raised here. Diversity, conceived as the nature of the universe itself, is not and should not be conceptualized as a problem. The real problem, one that educators should take with immense seriousness, is that there is often so much **disparity** within diverse contexts. Hence, it is not diversity that is the problem, but disparities. Sometimes, as in many countries at the beginning of this century, there are considerable academic disparities between and among ethnic groups such that there are large gaps between the academic performance of African American and Latino/Latina and white students in the United States; Maori and Pakeha children in New Zealand, native Fijian and Indian Fijian children in Fiji, or Han and national minority groups in China. Note here that dominant does not need to be in numeric terms; in Fiji, it is the Fijian Indian children who are in the numerical minority, but who, for historic political and geographic reasons, perform better at school. In some cases, disparities are evident in terms of disciplinary action, suspensions, streaming to vocational and/or lower level academic programs (and their counterpart programs for academically talented and gifted students). These are issues educators need to carefully consider. Perhaps a dose of Bakhtinian carnival would once again be useful to overthrow some preconceptions and traditions and introduce new ways of relating dialogically to one another. Remember Bakhtin's firm belief that a "carnival sense of the world possesses a mighty life-creating and transforming power, an indestructible vitality" (1984a, p. 107). Having some fun, introducing some unexpectedness into a situation can go a long way toward seeing people as equals, a prerequisite for overcoming disparity. In turn, this new awareness may be a catalyst for seriously addressing the underlying and persistent systemic issues.

A very simple example comes to mind. One year I had a graduate class in which several students were

Disparity

expresses the inequities that often accompany differences of age, rank, ethnicity, or socio-economic status

very vocal and many were virtually silent. Some but not all of the silent majority were international students for whom English was not their first language. At first, I tried preparing the silent students, suggesting they might want to consider a specific topic or reading so I could call on them during the next class. Although this tactic seemed to make them more comfortable when called on, it did nothing to encourage free discussion at other times.

After several weeks of trying to encourage the silent students to speak, I decided to try an experiment. I purchased a bag of wrapped chocolate candy and every time a student spoke, I tossed a candy in his or her direction. Suddenly, one student cried out, "If you talk you get a candy," and soon everyone was vying for the opportunity to talk and gain a reward. Remember this was a graduate class. My students were dedicated adult educators who could certainly have purchased whatever candy they wanted at any time. It was not the candy but the carnival that got their attention, the unanticipated throwing of candy by a professor in a graduate program. What struck me during the rest of the class was that those who had been silent became as loquacious as the others despite the continued absence of further rewards.

I recognize that explaining why some students were less vocal than others would require a complex and extensive analysis of the social makeup and power structures of the class. Silence cannot simply be attributed to personality or to lack of facility with the dominant language. However, for the purposes of this discussion, that is exactly the point. Regardless of what caused the silence, introducing carnival on a very temporary basis, permanently changed the interactions and relationships in the class.

The foregoing illustration should not be seen as a simple cause and effect prescription for making students talk. It does not address power imbalances that may exist in the class and which may be at the root of some students' reluctance to respond. It does not follow that every time a teacher throws candy students will respond. Further, there is absolutely no guarantee that once students have begun to respond in a class, they will continue to do so. In the foregoing illustration, a combination of surprise, anticipation, personalities, and previously developed relationships all contributed to creating a complex and somewhat carnivalesque atmosphere. The care with which the interactions were nourished, the continued teasing about the feverish response of adults to proffered candy, and the banter that followed all contributed to the continuation of both verbal participation and carnival in subsequent classes. Moreover, once the expectation for the unanticipated had been established, the students waited for the professor to engage in additional unusual behavior.

Toward Innovative and Novel Approaches to Schooling

As Schwartz and Ogilvy demonstrated with their 1979 research, we can no longer assume the neatness of simple cause and effect relationships when chaos and complexity theory have become the norm in most disciplines. Wheatley, in her 1998 book, *Leadership and the New Science,* prompted new ways of thinking about leadership. She introduced ideas from science and asked that we stop thinking about prediction and control which are never very effective in human organizations such as schools. Instead, she suggested we might focus on identifying and appreciating underlying patterns. She believed it was important for leaders to understand the relationships between simplicity and complexity. Simple equations, for example, when reproduced multiple times can lead to complex and intricate fractal designs. In like fashion, simple principles (not prescriptions) such as "engage in dialogic relationships," may guide complex organizations to more open, more complete, and more productive ways of operating.

At the same time, simplicity is not simple and should never be taken to imply that stereotypical or essentializing thinking is acceptable. Sadly, stereo-

types are particularly dominant in educational thought. Too often, when we seek to help teachers deal with a diverse student body, we generalize by making statements such as, "Indigenous students will not look you in the eye" or "Asian students are good at math," or "African American students are good at sports." The intent may be good, but the outcome is the development of programs and approaches that do little more than fulfill our stereotypical predictions.

Frequently our assumptions lead to deficit thinking, to a kind of pathologizing of children's lived experiences. For example we may assume children from certain ethnic groups, who speak a certain language, or who live in a particular area of town are less academically able or motivated than their peers whose home life is more traditionally middle class. Sometimes this leads to inaccurate and unwarranted assumptions about students' ability or about their behavior. Even after Dr. Ruth Simmons had been appointed as the first African American president of an Ivy League University, she reported to Morley Safer of CBS's *60 Minutes,* that when she shopped in stores such as Macy's in New York, she was followed and sometimes even stopped and searched by security guards. So ingrained were their assumptions about the socioeconomic level and concomitant behaviors of African American women, that they saw nothing but her skin color. In like fashion, we are often so blinded by the fact that a student is wearing dirty and ragged clothes that we fail to identify the quick mind and the curiosity with which he approaches learning. Taking a Bakhtinian approach, we would once again live dialogically, entering into the moment in relationship, and learning from the others with alternative perspectives. We would not dismiss them because of a superficial characteristic.

Living in Community

One implication of Bakhtin's novel approach to the world is the need to live in community. If two voices are necessary for life, if we live and grow only in interaction with other, "foreign" voices, then we

cannot put primacy on the individual. Living relationally and dialogically requires attending to communal life.

Sometimes one thinks of community as being relatively homogeneous, as in a religious community, a gated housing community, and so forth. Even here, there is diversity within apparent homogeneity. While there may be some common beliefs or values that draw people together, there are also many dissimilarities among them. People may choose to live in a particular community because they can afford a certain style of house, like a particular style of living (rural or suburban, for example); they may want their children to attend a certain school, or they may work for the same employer (as in those whose have enlisted in military service), yet at the same time, they may speak different languages, have differently configured families, choose various leisure activities, vacation in different places, and so forth.

Because communities are never homogeneous, several theorists write and speak about the concept of "communities of difference" (Shields, 2003) or communities of "otherness" (Furman, 1998). Such communities recognize difference is at the root of community and hence that there can be no pre-assumed norms, beliefs, and values to which members must subscribe in order to become "members"; instead, char-

Community of difference

refers to a heterogeneous community in which respect and dialogue help members to identify shared norms, beliefs, and values

acteristics of a **community of difference** emerge from the ongoing and deeply respectful interaction of all participants. These ideas are consistent with a Bakhtinian universe in which one does not start from an assumption of shared norms, beliefs, or values into which the other must "fit," but with an assumption of openness and heteroglossia, from which community must emerge.

Bakhtin suggested that to live fully in the intersection of time and space, we need to live life as constituted by the public square of ancient times. This is a helpful way for the educator to think of a school—as a site in which the public may come together, bringing their differences of perspectives, cultures, and languages to debate, to discuss, and to decide

together what the norms, rules, and processes of the organization will be. Here, there is no sense that one group has a pre-ordinate claim to the rights and responsibilities of participation, but that people work out how to live together in harmony and shared citizenship.

When educators think seriously about the nature of the spaces in which learning and sense-making occur, it is apparent that even young children may learn to participate in community life. Schools do not have to be authoritarian, monologic places in which children passively respond to instructions of adults. Such activities as community clean-ups, town hall meetings, student led parent-teacher conferences, student leadership and mediation activities, meaningful student governance, and open-ended pedagogical activities all help to create a sense of community in which people feel ownership and acceptance.

Moving Toward "Truth"

As discussed in earlier chapters, for Bakhtin, multiple voices and diverse perspectives never merge to provide a total or final insight one might call "truth." Rather, truth, as he used the term, is to be found, not in individual inquiry, not in randomized, replicable, empirical research studies, but in the communal and collective search for meaning. We recall his assertion that

> the truth is not born and does not reside in the head of an individual person; it is born of the dialogical intercourse *between people* in the collective search for truth. (1973, p. 90)

This is consistent, too, as we saw, with Palmer's definition of truth as "*an eternal conversation about things that matter, conducted with passion and discipline*" (1998, p. 104).

If educators accept this concept of truth as a collective inquiry and ongoing conversation, one that must have multiple voices in order for "truth" to emerge, it could change the ways in which we think about both educational research and daily practice. There is no sense that we must come to a resolution, a compromise, but that in order for truth to emerge, one must somehow learn to "hear and comprehend both or all voices simultaneously" (Sidorkin, 1999, p. 30). The implications for how we teach and test are enormous. Instead of teaching students, there is one correct and pre-determined response, educators could focus on spaces in which sense-making conversations and dialogue could occur. Instead of pushing aside conversation, for example, about the rightness or wrongness of publishing cartoons depicting Mohamed, such conversations would be encouraged in order to promote understanding, although not necessarily resolution, of the issue.

Bakhtin stated that

> a dialogue of languages is a dialogue of social forces perceived not only in their static co-existence, but also as a dialogue of different times, epochs, and days, a dialogue that is forever dying, living, being born: co-existence and becoming are fused into an indissoluble concrete unity that is contradictory, multi-speeched and heterogeneous. (1981d, p. 365)

When we teach as though all information were discrete and static, we fail to bring into existence the new dialogues that create the best possible, multi-speeched, and heterogeneous "truth." Conversely, when we teach students to recognize the alternative perspectives present in all of the subject matter that constitutes the formal curriculum, we are teaching in an open and dialogic fashion. To do so might require, for example, teachers of literature to introduce texts (including visuals) that help students learn about different cultures, customs, and ways of life. Teachers of social studies and history would encourage debate about contested and controversial notions such as citizenship, terrorism, or national security. Such dialogues would not be confined to those "traditional" subject areas, however, but spaces for dialogue would be infused into all subject areas. In a math or science class, studying stress or force related to the creation of a large hydro-electric dam would lead naturally to an exploration of the possible advantages and disadvantages of the dam's likely environ-

mental and social impact. Moreover, terms such as "impact" or "citizenship" would also be recognized as complex, contested notions. Consider, for example, the nature of citizenship in a country like the United States. What rights are implied and for whom? Do those who have immigrated and acquired citizenship have the same rights as those born in the country—regardless of the color of their skin or of their parents' origin? Do all those born in the country have equal rights and access to goods such as health care or to processes such as voting?

In the current climate of educational accountability, we focus more on test scores than truth, on right answers more than on multiple interpretations, on solutions more than on questions. In doing so, we once again narrow rather than enlarge the learning that occurs within schools. We constrain the life-giving voices that are inherent in our heteroglossic world, reducing them to something manageable rather than understandable, and we prevent teachers and students alike from learning in the joyful freedom of carnival in which barriers are torn down and life is renewed.

Thinking about "truth" in a Bakhtinian sense, rather than as information that is fixed, inviolable, and replicable on tests, frees teachers and students for the tasks of exploration and sense-making that can constitute schooling as exciting, relevant, and meaningful rather than staid, boring, irrelevant, and meaningless.

Putting It Together: An Ontological Approach

When I think of education that is Bakhtinian in nature, I think most often of the kaleidoscope I purchased from an artist last summer and which sits in a prominent place on the living room coffee table in my new home. Its form is defined, but within the "box" there is a constant and glorious movement of patterns, all constructed of elements that in themselves do not change except in relation to one another. One moment, the images suggest a magical flower; the next, a magnificent sunset; and the next, the

grandeur of the stained glass windows of the Sainte Chapelle in Paris. There is not Truth, but there are *truths*. Every time one picks it up, there is new insight, new images, new meaning. It is never ending, never finished. There is, and can be, no "last word."

In contrast, consider the monoscope. It is an instrument through which one looks at an unchanging world in static ways. No matter who picks it up, no matter how one looks through it, the image is inert, fixed. There is no movement, no color. Only one interpretation is possible. When one looks at the red rocks and desert terrain of world-famed Monument Valley, Utah, there is no play of light or shadow on the red rock buttes regardless of the season or the time of day. As one climbs into a canyon and comes across a ruin or some petroglyphs, they speak for themselves. There can be no interpretation, changing over time, about the ancient workers, or about the meanings of the symbols. Everything is fixed— regardless of the onlooker, his or her training, or the time and culture in which he or she lives.

It must be clear at this point that the monoscope is in reality a figment of my imagination.[4] Reality is not static, fixed for all time, unchanged and unchanging. Yet, so often, the ways in which we talk about education—in terms of structures, roles, curriculum, testing, discipline and so forth—all seem to imply that there can be such a closed and finalized approach to educating children, youths, and even adults in formal systems and institutions of schooling.

These implications have led to practices that are not only surprisingly widespread but which are also generally recognized as ineffective. Much has been written in recent years about the failure of schools and school systems in many countries to reduce the gap between minoritized and majority students, between marginalized and dominant groups. There has been considerable critique of curricular programs that tend to deskill teachers, purporting to be "best practice" rather than fostering the ability to adapt what and how they teach according to the subject

at hand and the needs of the student. There have been critical assessments of the failure of multicultural or anti-racist programs to combat systemic and endemic racism; with some suggesting that the more exposure people have received to such approaches, the more racism has been moved into silenced and covert practices.

I am not positing that adopting some of Bakhtin's principles would be a panacea to cure the ills of society or the ills of education. I am not advocating that we develop, market, and implement Bakhtinian educational reform. Indeed, nothing could be less consistent with his concepts of chronotope, heteroglossia, dialogue, and carnival. Taking a Bakhtinian approach is not simply another new recipe or program. It is not a set of precepts or principles to follow. However, permitting his worldview and ideas to inform us would be a significant step in revitalizing and transforming education.

Bakhtin suggests an ontological approach—one that takes difference and heteroglossia as foundational to life itself. Life as he comprehends it is vibrant, open, fluid, and temporary. Education, if it is to truly bring people to a fullness of life, should also be vibrant, exciting, challenging, and open, with the goal of deeper understanding rather than rigid knowing.

Recent experiences in my own life have convinced me that the need for some dramatic new ways of thinking about education is perhaps greater than ever before. Watching and discussing the 2005 Academy-award winning film *Crash* with friends reminded me once again of the complexities of race and prejudice, and perhaps even more importantly of the difficulty of taking a definitive stand on certain issues. Helping people to have dialogue about such central topics both with others, and internally, rather than silencing debate about critical issues out of fear of losing control would be consistent with Bakhtin's writing.

I have watched, with the rest of the world, as violence has continued to erupt in countries such as

Iraq, Pakistan, Sudan, and Haiti. Yet I have frequently been in uncomfortable situations in which people make authoritative statements that go unchallenged—statements in which one political, ethnic, or religious group is blamed for what is certainly a historically complex and currently difficult situation without such clear-cut responses. Situations like these seem to occur with such regularity that I wonder why we do not consider it of central and utmost importance to teach students of all ages to raise questions that challenge simplistic and prejudicial thinking.

Recently, for example, two very short exchanges reminded me once again of the need to create spaces in which such dialogue occurs. I raised with colleagues a request from an administrator from an institution from an Islamic country to meet with us in the hope of establishing an academic partnership, only to have the initial flippant response be, "We might have to deal with Al Quaida!" The second occurred when I went to lunch with a group of people who were recruiting a new colleague, and the conversation turned to a discussion about the safety of the community. "There really is little crime," one asserted, "but when I first moved here twenty years ago I wished I had a gun. A group of Arabs moved into the apartment across the hall and I was so afraid they were terrorists, I made sure I only entered or left my suite when I was sure I would not encounter them." The conversation quickly moved on, with no one but me apparently disturbed by the prejudice implied by such statements, until I laughingly stammered, "I suppose you later discovered they were all medical students!"

I am not suggesting that a large formal meal is always the best place to raise such questions, to challenge monologic interpretations, or to attempt to create an understanding of outsidedness or dialogue. Such comments, though, reflect attitudes which beg to be addressed no matter how difficult or uncomfortable it may seem at first. Moreover, I am arguing for an education system that prepares us to do so, one that creates spaces in which students of all ages learn

to engage others respectfully and safely, but in which fixed, authoritarian, and monologic expressions of prejudice are no longer the norm.

Bakhtin introduces a whole new way of thinking and living. The ideas we have explored in this primer are not new prescriptions, new programs, or new skills that can be taught to educators going through teacher or administrator preparation programs in our colleges and universities. They cannot be legislated by policy makers nor evaluated through the use of new and improved standardized assessments of educators or students.

This exploration of some of the major themes that run through Bakhtin's work suggests a novel, ontological approach. *Chronotope* is not a fixed point on a map or a calendar but a new and more connected way of thinking about the interplay of time and space, of social and historic forces. *Heteroglossia* is not a poster on a wall with people of different colors holding hands but a way of acknowledging the fundamental diversity of the universe. *Dialogue* is not just talk but a way of engaging diversity and of developing new understandings. *Carnival* is not a planned social event but a joyful and spontaneous way of introducing new power dynamics and alternative approaches to institutional life. Taken together, these four major concepts and themes imply new ways of teaching, learning, leading, and living.

The key is an ontological approach. Bakhtin calls us to live life as an exciting journey, always unfinished, always open to new ideas, new ways of thinking or acting, never totally constrained by hierarchies, rules, roles, attitudes, or expectations. At the same time, he never advocates anarchy. He recognizes repeatedly that carnival is not a permanent situation but a temporary disruption, albeit one that likely has a long lasting impact. He calls us to live in dialogue, acknowledging that in dialogue is the only "truth" to be found in human exploration and interaction. Most importantly, he calls us to live joyfully, respectfully, wholly in open relation to others, recognizing that nothing is final or complete. The word, the relationship, the idea, the knowledge, the understanding, the insight may have come to a temporary resting place, but they are never finished. So, too, our life and work . . . !

GLOSSARY

Community of Difference—refers to a heterogeneous community in which respect and dialogue help members to identify shared norms, beliefs, and values to guide the conduct of the community as a whole. It is in contrast to fixed and homogeneous community in which to belong, one must accept existing norms without discussion or opportunity to influence them.

Contextualizing—taking account of context, rejecting a "one size fits all" approach, and recognizing that differences in values and perspectives make a difference to what is acceptable and valuable to a given group of people.

Disparity—expresses the inequities that often accompany differences of age, rank, ethnicity, or socio-economic status. It often results because of power imbalances and hierarchical structures.

Dynamic learning—implies that what we learn and accept as "truth" or "fact" at one time may change as new knowledge, discoveries, and understandings come to the fore.

Minoritized—refers to the marginalizing and subordinate treatment of a group expressing ideas, beliefs, or behaviors that contradict the dominant norms of an organization. Minoritized groups are not necessarily the numerical minority. For example, in a school with a 60% Native American population, the indigenous students may still be marginalized due to the dominance of white, middle-class cultural perspectives in the curriculum.

Transmission-oriented pedagogy—refers to a form of instruction according to which it is the task of the teacher to "tell" or "transmit" information seen as fixed and factual. It is in contrast to current constructivist and constructionist approaches to teaching in which knowledge is seen as co-constructed.

NOTES

1   I have chosen to name the school after Bep-Kororoti, a mythical space warrior worshipped by the tribes of the upper reaches of the Xing River. The school is actually named after an astronaut,

but to maintain confidentiality I have selected the mythical name. This use of a pseudonym emphasizes that it is not my intent to glorify any one school, but to suggest ways in which education may be more consistent with Bakhtin's worldview—even within a large public school system.

2   It must be noted that ability to pay was addressed by the school, and those who cannot afford to pay are provided "scholarships" or assistance by the school and district.

3   For a more complete discussion of Palmer's paradoxes, please see Fraser & Shields, 2006

4   Interestingly, however, the concept was attempted at one point. The term was used to describe a black, gray, and white test pattern of the B/W television era intended to provide a constant, fixed, and unchanging focal point against which viewers could test their television adjustments. It "was precisely etched into a CRT, thus did not require external lighting, focus or keystone adjustment." Interestingly, it failed because it was not as static and fixed as had been hoped; "and to make matters worse, the adjustments for these parameters often interacted with picture size and position, so that optimum correction was a compromise at best." In other words, it did not work (see Monoscope, 2006).

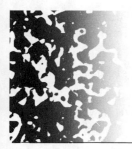

References

Cited in This Volume

Agora. (2005). Plate-forme de gestion de contenu. Service d'information du gouvernement. http://www.agora.gouv.fr/

The American Heritage® Dictionary of the English Language, 4th ed. Boston: Houghton Mifflin Company.

Bakhtin, M. M. (1973). *Problems of Dostoevsky's poetics*. Ann Arbor, MI: Ardis.

Bakhtin, M. M. (1981a). Epic and novel: Toward a Methodology for the study of the novel. In *The dialogic imagination*. (Caryl Emerson & Michael Holquist, Trans.) (pp. 3–40). Austin, TX: University of Texas Press.

Bakhtin, M. M. (1981b). From the prehistory of novelistic discourse. In *The dialogic imagination*. (Caryl Emerson & Michael Holquist,Ttrans.) (pp. . 41–83). Austin, TX: University of Texas Press.

Bakhtin, M. M. (1981c). Forms of time and of the chronotope in the novel: Notes toward a historical poetics. In *The dialogic imagination* (Caryl Emerson & Michael Holquist, Trans.) (pp. 84–258). Austin, TX: University of Texas Press.

Bakhtin, M. M. (1981d). Discourse in the novel. In *The dialogic imagination*. (Caryl Emerson & Michael Holquist, Trans.) (pp. 259–422). Austin, TX: University of Texas Press.

Bakhtin, M. M. (1984a). *The problems of Dostoevsky's poetics*. Minneapolis, MN: University of Minnesota Press.

Bakhtin, M. M. (1984b). *Rabelais and his world* (H. Iswolsky, Trans.). Bloomington, IN: Indiana University Press.

Bakhtin, M. M. (1986a). Response to a question from the *Novy Mir* editorial staff. In C. Emerson & M. Holquist (Eds.), *Speech genres and other late essays*, (M. Holquist, Trans.) (pp. 1–9). Austin, TX: University of Texas Press.

Bakhtin, M. M. (1986b). The problem of speech genres. In C. Emerson & M. Holquist (Eds.), *Speech genres and other late essays*. (V. W. Mcgee, Trans.) (pp. 60–102). Austin, TX: University of Texas Press.

Bakhtin, M. M. (1986c). The problem of the text. In C. Emerson & M. Holquist (Eds.), *Speech genres and other late essays* (V. W. Mcgee, Trans.) (pp. 103–131). Austin, TX: University of Texas Press.

Bakhtin, M. M. (1986d). From notes made in 1970–71. *Speech genres and other late essays* (V. W. Mcgee, Trans.). In C. Emerson & M. Holquist (Eds.), (pp. 132–158). Austin, TX: University of Texas Press.

Bakhtin, M. M. (1986e). Toward a methodology for the human sciences, (V. W. Mcgee, Trans.). In C. Emerson & M. Holquist (Eds.), *Speech genres and other late essays* (pp. 159–172). Austin, TX: University of Texas Press.

Barnard, C. I. (1938). *The functions of the executive*. Cambridge, MA: Harvard University Press.

Boler, M. (2004). All speech is not free: The ethics of affirmative action pedagogy. In M. Boler (Ed.), *Democratic dialogue in education* (pp. 3–14) New York: Peter Lang.

Booth, W. C. (1984). Introduction. In M. M. Bakhtin (C. Emerson Ed. & Trans), *Problems of Dostoevsky's poetics*. Minneapolis, MN: University of Minnesota Press.

Bourdieu, P. (1990). *The logic of practice*. Oxford: Polity Press.

Buber, M. (1970). *I and Thou*. (W. Kaufman, Trans). New York: Charles Scribner & Sons.

Burbules, N. C. (1993). *Dialogue in teaching*. New York: Teachers College Press.

Caine, G., & Caine, R. N. (1994). *Making connections: Teaching and the human brain*. Alexandria, VA: ASCD.

Cuban, L. (1990). Reforming again, again, and again. *Educational Researcher, 19*(1), 3–13.

Cummins, J. (1989) Empowering minority students: A framework for intervention. In N. M. Hidalgo, C. L. McDowell, & E. V. Siddle (Eds.), *Facing racism in education* (pp. 50–68). Cambridge, MA: Harvard Educational Review *Reprint Series 21.*

Delpit, L. D. (1988). The silenced dialogue: Power and pedagogy in educating other people's children. *Harvard Educational Review, 58*(3): 280–298.

Douglas-Hall, A., & Koball, H. (2004). Low-income children in the United States. New York: National Center for Children in Poverty. Accessed November 22, 2005 at http://www.nccp.org/.

Emerson, C. (1984). Editor's preface. In M. Bakhtin (Emerson, C., Trans. & Ed.), *Problems of Dostoevsky's Poetics.* Minneapolis, MN: University of Minnesota Press.

Farrell, J. P. (1999). Changing conceptions of equality of education: Forty years of comparative evidence. In R. F. Arnove & C. A. Torres (Eds.), *Comparative education: The dialectic of the global and the local* (pp. 149–177). Lanham, MD: Rowman & Littlefield.

Fraser, D., & Shields, C. M. (20060. Spiritual daring, paradox, and educational leadership. *New Zealand Journal of Educational Leadership, 21* (1).

Fraser, N. (1995). From redistribution to recognition? Dilemmas of justice in a 'post-socialist' age. *New Left Review, (212,:* 568–593.

Fullan, M. (1999). *Change forces: The sequel.* New York: Falmer.

Furman, G. C. (1998). Postmodernism and community in schools: Unraveling the paradox. *Educational Administration Quarterly, 34(*3), 298–328.

Gadamer, H.G. (2002). *Truth and method.* (2nd, rev,ed.). (J. Weinsheimer & D. Marshall, Trans.). New York: Continuum.

Gardner, H. (1983). *Frames of mind: The theory of multiple intelligences.* New York: Basic Books.

Garrison, J. (2004). Ameliorating violence in dialogues across differences: The role of eros and logos. In M. Boler (Ed.), *Democratic dialogue in education* (pp. 89103). New York: Peter Lang.

Glass, R. D. (2004). Moral and political clarity and education as a practice of freedom. In M. Boler (Ed.), *Democratic dialogue in education* (pp. 16–32). New York: Peter Lang.

Gould, S. J. (1981). *The mismeasure of man.* New York: W. W. Norton & Co.

Grumet, M. R. (1995). The curriculum: What are the basics and are we teaching them? In J. L. Kincheloe & S. R. Steinberg (Eds.), *Thirteen questions.* 2nd ed. (pp.15–21). New York: Peter Lang.

Hamilton, J. (2005). *The balanced calendar school: A continuous learning opportunity*. Brampton, ON: Peel School District.

Harris, J. L. (2005). Grace under pressure: Business etiquette strategies for women. *Palm Beach Post*. Accessed November 24, 2005 at http://www.palmbeachclassifieds.com/employment/jobs/main/jobs_dressscode_main.html.

Hellenic Ministry of Culture. (2001). *The ancient agora of Athens*. Accessed April 2006 at http://www.culture.gr/2/21/211/21101a/e211aa03.html.

Holquist, M. (1981). Introduction. In M. Holquist (Ed.), *The dialogic imagination*. (C. Emerson & M. Holquist, Trans.), Austin, TX: University of Texas Press.

Holquist, M. (1986). Introduction. In C. Emerson & M. Holquist (Eds.), *Speech genres and other late essays* (M. Holquist, Trans.). Austin, TX: University of Texas Press.

Janis, I. L. (1982). *Groupthink. Psychological studies of policy decisions and fiascoes*. New York: Houghton Mifflin.

Jensen, E. (1995). *Brain-based learning*. San Diego, CA: The Brain Store.

Jones, N. A. (2005). *We the people of more than one race in the United States*. Census 2000 special reports; issued April 2005. U.S. Census Bureau. Accessed April 2006 at www.census.gov/prod/2005pubs/censr-22.pdf.

Levine, A. (2005). *Educating school leaders*. The education schools project. Washington, DC. Accessed April 2006 at http://www.edschools.org/reports_leaders.htm.

Majority-Minority State. (2005). Wikipedia: The free encyclopedia. Accessed November 22, 2005 at http://en.wikipedia.org/wiki/Majority-minority_state

Meyer, J. W., & Rowan, B. (1977). Institutionalized organizations: Formal structure as myth and ceremony. *The American Journal of Sociology, 83*(2), 340–363.

Monoscope. (http://www.r-vcr.com/~television/TV/monoscope.htm). Accessed February 23, 2006.

Morris, P. (1994). Introduction. In P. Morris (Ed.), *The Bakhtin reader*. New York: Edward Arnold/Hodder Headline Group.

Ogbu, J. (1992). Understanding cultural diversity and learning. *Educational Researcher, 21*(8), 5–14.

Ogawa, R. T. (2005). Leadership as a social construct: The expression of human agency within organizational constraint. In F, W, English (Ed.), *The Sage handbook of educational leadership: Advances in theory, research, and practice* (pp. 89–108). Thousand Oaks, CA: SAGE.

Palmer, P. J. (1998). *The courage to teach.* San Francisco, CA: Jossey-Bass.

Pope, A. (1951). Essay on criticism. In E. F. Kingston (Ed.), *Poems to remember* (pp. 188–189). Toronto, Ontario, Canada: J. M. Dent & Sons. (Original work published 1711)

Restak, R. M. (1984). *The brain.* New York: Bantam.

Rostel, R. W. (1973). Translation of M. M. Bakhtin *Problems of Dostoevsky's poetics.* Ann Arbor, MI: Ardis.

Schwartz, P., & Ogilvy, J. (1979). *The emergent paradigm: Changing patterns of thought and belief.* Menlo Park, CA: SRI International.

Senge, P. (1990). The fifth discipline: The art and practice of the learning organization. New York: Doubleday/Currency.

Shavelson, R. J., & Towne, L. (Eds.). (2002). *Scientific research in education.* Committee on Scientific Principles for Education Research. Center for Education. Division of Behavioral and Social Sciences and Education. National Research Council. Washington, DC: National Academy Press. Accessed April 2006 at http://www.nap.edu/execsumm/0309082919.html

Sher, P. (2002). From carnival to carnival. *Cabinet, 6, spring.* Accessed July 2006 at http://cabinetmagazine.org/issues/6/carnival.php

Shields, C. M. (2002). *Understanding the challenges; exploring the opportunities, and developing new understandings: Examining the effects of the past four years.* Report prepared for the San Juan County Board of Education, Utah.

Shields, C. M. (2003). *Good intentions are not enough: Transformative leadership for communities of difference.* Lanham, MD: Scarecrow.

Shields, C. M., & Edwards, M. M. (2005). *Dialogue is not just talk: A new ground for educational leaders.* New York: Peter Lang.

Sidorkin, A. M. (1999). *Beyond discourse: Education, the self, and dialogue.* Albany, NY: State University of New York Press.

Sidorkin, A. M. (2002). *Learning relations.* New York: Peter Lang.

Starratt, R. J. (2005). The spirituality of presence for educational leaders. In C. M. Shields, M. M. Edwards, & A. Sayani (Eds.). *Inspiring practice: Spirituality and educational leadership* (pp. 67–84). Lancaster, PA: Pro>Active.

Steinbeck, J. (1993). *Of mice and men.* New York: Penguin. (Original work published 1937)

Swartz, D. (1997). *Culture and power: The Sociology of Pierre Bourdieu.* Chicago: University of Chicago Press.

U.S. Census Bureau, Census 2000, Summary File 3, Table PCT 10, Internet release data, February 25, 2003, http://www.census.gov/population/cen2000/phc-t20/tab05.pdf

Voltaire. (1759). *Candide*. Accessed April 2006. Available at http://eserver.org/fiction/candide.txt.

Vygotsky, L. S. (1978). *Mind and society: The development of higher mental processes*. Cambridge, MA: Harvard University Press.

Webster's new millennium dictionary of English. (2003–2005). Los Angeles, CA: Lexico Publishing Group. Accessed November 24, 2005 as www.dictionary.com.

Wheatley, M. (1993). *Leadership and the new science*. San Francisco: Berrett-Koehler.

www.adherents Accessed November 22, 2005 at http://www.adherents.com/rel_USA.html#religions

Other Works About Bakhtin

Although there are dozens of works about Bakhtin, there are virtually none that relate to education in general. Some focus on the literary implications of his work; others identify particular literary subjects to whom the analysis might apply. I have listed here a few general works that the reader might find of assistance in thinking further about the application of the ideas I have introduced to teaching, pedagogy, educational leadership, and the organization of schooling.

Hirschlop, K., & Shepherd, D. (Eds.). (1989). *Bakhtin and cultural theory*. Manchester, UK: Manchester University Press.

Morson, G. S., & Emerson, C. (1989). *Rethinking Bakhtin*. Evanston, IL: Northwestern University Press.

Shires, Jeff (n.d.). *A bibliography of works by and about the Bakhtinian Circle* accessed April 2006 at http://www.geocities.com/CollegePark/Campus/8297/bakhtin.html.

Sidorkin, A. M. (1997). Carnival and domination: Pedagogies of neither care nor justice. *Educational Theory, 47*(2), 229–239.

Swingewood, A. (1998). *Cultural theory and the problem of modernity*. New York: St. Martin's.

Toohey, K., Waterstons, B., & Julé-Lemke, A. (2000). Community of learners, carnival, and participation in a Punjabi Sikh classroom. *The Canadian Modern Language Review, 56*(3), 421–436.

The University of Sheffield: The Bakhtin Centre http://www.shef.ac.uk/bakhtin/ Vice, S. (1997). *Introducing Bakhtin*. New York: Palgrave.

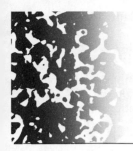

Index

9/11 (September 11, 2001), 30, 50

absolute past, 18
action, 25, 66, 72, 90, 91, 93
adventure time, 7, 12-13, 32, 137
African American, 21, 25, 60, 71
agency, 7-8, 12, 16, 24, 32, 120, 136-140, 142, 149
agora, 33, 102, (*see also* public square)
Alexander Pope, 69
ambiguous unity, 150-152
American Heritage Dictionary, 107
Amita, 73-75, 81-82, 115
Asian, 25, 27, 60, 62, 168, 170
authoritarian voice, 31, 40, 61, 86, 93, 154 (*see also* authority)
authority, 9, 17, 19, 25, 27, 32, 119, 144, 156, 160
Bakhtin, the man, 3-6
Bakhtinian Circle, 5
balanced calendar, 23, 130, 131, 142

best practice, 1, 12, 16, 68, 100, 146, 164, 173
binary thinking, 1
biographical time, 14, 32, 137
bi-racial, 22, (*see also* multi-ethnic)
Boler, 88
Booth, 4, 6, 30
Bourdieu, 3, 20, 23, 32, 97, 142
brain-based learning, 71
Brown vs. the Board of Education, 20-21
Buber, 64-64, 72-73, 162
Buddhism/Buddhist, 12
Canada, 75-76, 88, 153
carnival misalliances, 102, 105
carnival, 1, 9-11, 32, 63, 95, 97-128, 130-131, 133, 143-145, 161-162, 165-167, 172, 174, 176

cartoons, 37, 148,
census, 17, 22, 182-183
centrifugal forces, 15, 32, 47

centripetal forces, 15-16, 32, 47, 48

charter schools, 164

Chester Barnard, 27

Christian/ity, 17, 56, 60, 78, 84, 96

chronotope, 1, 6-8, 10-12, 15, 17, 25, 31, 32, 36, 39, 63, 70, 109, 114, 120, 125, 127, 130, 135, 137, 140, 145, 148, 150, 155, 174, 176

color-blind(ness), 160

Columbus Day, 25

communication, 2, 9-10, 19, 27, 33, 49, 102-103, 105, 109-111, 125, 127, 130, 138, 161

community, 8, 14, 16, 28-29, 32-33, 79-80, 89-90, 92-94, 131-132, 146-147, 151, 155, 164, 168-170, 175, 177

community of difference, 169, 177

complexity, 7, 15, 32, 41, 86, 100, 136, 151, 156-158, 167

conflict/conflicting/conflictual, 1-2, 9, 33, 36, 39, 47, 54-55, 61, 80, 90-94, 111, 116

context, 7-8, 12-16, 19-20, 31-32, 37, 39, 42-47, 49, 57, 66-67, 70, 110, 116, 120, 123, 127, 133, 152, 154-156, 158, 159

Courtenay, 112-113

craniometric studies, 70

Crash, 174

Cuban, 3

culture, cultural, 4-6, 8-9, 15, 23-24, 26, 33, 35, 37, 44, 49-59, 66, 74-76, 79, 95, 102, 108, 111, 114, 116, 118, 121-122, 130-131, 134, 138, 141-142, 146-147, 155-157, 169, 171, 173

Cummins, 19, 146

curriculum, 2, 13, 17, 22, 58, 100, 108-109, 131, 139, 158, 164, 171, 173

death, 103, 107, 108, 112, 113, 116, 124, 128, 145

deficit thinking, 16, 86, 91, 125, 168

Delpit, 43, 147

deskill, 13, 173

dialogic relations, 66-68, 72-74, 75, 95, 161, 165, 167

dialogic relationship, 66-67, 68, 72-74, 77, 161, 167

dialogism, 9-11, 40, 63-96, 135-136, 145, 147-148, (*see also* dialogue)

dialogue, 1, 9-11, 14-15, 32, 36, 40, 56, 59, 61, 63-96, 134-135, 141, 148-149, 151-152, 158-159, 169, 171, 174-177, (*see also* inner dialogue)

difference, 8, 9, 12, 17, 29, 32, 63, 66, 72, 74, 82, 92, 100, 128, 169, 174, 177

discrimination, 25, 37

disparity, 9, 165, 177

diversity, 9, 20, 29, 48, 55, 113, 134, 136, 147, 151, 152, 161, 163-165, 169, 176

dogma/dogmatism, 92-93, 95, 112, 121, 126, 147-148

Dostoevsky, 4-5, 36, 39, 99, 101, 119

Douglas-Hall & Koball, 16

dynamic tension, 28

eccentricity, 102, 106

education, 153

educational leadership, 2-4, 75, 128, 135,

educational praxis, 3

elite/elitism, 118, 128, 156

Emerson, 7

epic past, 18, 22

epic time, 19

essentialize/essentializing, 36, 51, 61, 167

ethnicity, 24, 37, 56, 91

ethnocentricism/ethnocentric, 47, 61

experimentation, 17

Foucault, 3

fourth dimension, 11

Fraser, 138

freedom, 5, 18, 87, 104, 107, 114, 122, 125, 137, 148-151, 164, 172
Fullan, 68
Furman, 169

Gadamer, 69
Galen, 70
garish dress, 44
Garrison, 72
generation gap, 50
Glass, 94
Gould, 71
Greece, 102
grotesque, 102, 106-109, 124, 128
groupthink, 87
Grumet, 17, 139

habitus, 20, 22-23, 32-33, 97, 136, 142-143
Hamilton, 133
handshake, 46-47
hegemony/hegemonic, 31, 56, 160
heteroglossia, 1, 8—10, 31, 33, 36, 39, 47-48, 51-52, 55-56, 59-61, 63, 66, 69, 79-80, 83, 91-92, 95, 100, 125, 127, 135, 145, 159, 163, 169, 172, 174, 176
hierarchy/hierarchical, 10, 18-20, 25, 32-33, 80, 93, 97-102, 104-106, 109, 119-120, 126, 136, 161-162, 176
Hinduism/Hindu, 13, 75, 134
Hmong, 47
Holbein, 107
holidays, 56
Holquist, 4, 48, 161
horizon, 69

ideology/ideological, 22, 46, 49-54, 60
immigration, 21, 76
incompleteness, 28, 136, 140, 152-155
inconclusive/ness, 28, 31
individual consciousness, 72, 80, 163

individualism, 92
inequity/inequitable, 10, 21, 32, 97, 103, 121, 138, 165, 177
inner dialogue, 15, 66, 83-84, 87, 89-90, 95
inquiry, 3-4, 80, 83, 89, 136, 140-141, 151, 160, 170
inter-racial, 22, 86
introspection, 14, 22-23, 25, 37
Islam, see Muslim

Jensen, 71
Jones, 22

kaleidoscope, 172
Kayser, 107
Kororoti Elementary School, 129-135
language, 35-36, 38-45, 47-51, 53-59, 63-64, 66, 69, 83-84, 93-94, 102, 109-114, 146-147, 153, 161, 171
laughter, 77, 103, 107, 111, 120-124, 126-127, 159
learning, 1, 3, 7, 9, 11-12, 14-16, 18-19, 22, 24, 27, 39, 33, 48, 55, 58, 91, 95, 109, 113-114, 122-128, 131-132, 136, 138-147, 153, 155-159
  contextualized, see context
  dynamic 153, 177
Levine, 2
liberation, 94, 104, 110-111, 114
linguistics, 35, 39, 157
listen(ing), 8, 56-60, 86, 147-149, 151, 158-159
literary criticism, 6
logic of confidence, 149
loophole, 59-61

Maori, 46, 153, 165
Mardi Gras, 118
marionettes, 102, 114-118
masks, 102, 105-106, 114-118, 124, 128
mastery, 136, 140, 141
McLuhan, 45
medieval carnival, 9, 98, 99, 101, 125
mehndi/henna, 134-135

middle class, 17, 24, 108, 168, 177
Middle East, 47, 50
minoritized, 24, 147, 173, 177, (*see also* minority)
minority, 17, 25, 29, 51, 56, 146-147, 152, 164-165, 177, (*see also* minoritized)
miscegenation, 22
modernism, 68,
monoglot, 39
monologic/monological, 9, 38-40, 58, 61, 66-67, 82, 93, 97, 136, 145-148, 163, 170, 175-176
monologism, 10, 31, 40, 61, 145, 149
moral certainty, 94-95
moral life, 15, 66, 82-90, 150-151
Morris, 5, 45, 65
multiculturalism, 20, 22, 47, 174
multi-ethnic, 22
multiple intelligences, 71
multiple perspectives, 17, 40, 60, 154, 158
multi-racial, 22
Muslim, 13, 29-30, 37, 47, 51, 56, 60, 75-76, 87, 134, 148, 159

narratives of identity, 37-38
National Science Foundation, 3
Native American, 36, 88, 153, (see also Navajo)
Navajo, 53-55, 76, 156
New Zealand, 46, 88, 127, 143, 165
No Child Left Behind, 12, 138
norms, 20, 23, 29, 32-33, 74, 87, 93, 95, 101, 105, 108-109, 142, 144-145, 147, 149, 156, 169-170, 177

Ogawa, 138
Ogbu, 25
ontology/ontological, 9, 33, 61-62, 64-65, 91, 100, 135, 172-176
openness, 9, 38, 65, 73, 77, 90, 91, 96, 141, 159-161, 169

opposites, (the role of) 103, 124-125
oppositional voices, 88
outsidedness, 10, 75-76, 114, 136, 141-143, 159

Palestine/Palestinian, 51, 152
Palmer, 17, 79, 80, 89, 148, 151, 154, 170
parody, 103, 114, 123, 127-128
pathologize/pathologizing, 24, 168
pedagogy, 17, 33, 71, 88, 131, 144, 146, 164, 177
  constructivist, 177
  transmission oriented, 146

Plato, 79
pluralism, 13, 33, 40, 61
political correctness, 29, 81
polyglossia, 48, 56, (*see also* polyphony)
polyglot, 39, 48, 62, 161, (*see also* polyphony)
polyphonic, 39, 59-61, 66, 81, 88, 92, 147, (*see also* polyphony)
polyphony, 15, 31, 36, 39-40, 47-56, 62, 79, 81, 93, 100, 145, 159, 161
postmodern, 92, 78
poverty, 16, 24, 37, 81, 108, 137
power, 7-8, 10, 19, 21, 32, 36, 40,43, 52, 58, 62, 64, 97-98, 101-104, 107, 113-115, 118-123, 125, 137-138, 146-147, 160-161, 165-166, 176-177
power relations, 10, 19, 32, 120
praxis, 2, 3, 33
prejudice, 24, 73, 76-77, 86, 88, 91, 174-5, 176
public square, 8, 14, 33, 101-102, 125-126, 169, (*see also* agora)

Rabelais, 4-5, 101, 107
reflection, 14-16, 25, 28, 32, 59, 156
reflective/reflexivity, 31, 130, 136, 156-159
regeneration, 103, 117, 121, 125

relational/relationality, 44, 64-65, 136, 161-162, 169
relationship, 64, 72, 105, 161-162
relativism, 147-148, 92, 96
religion, 23, 30, 32, 51, 56
resistance, 13
ritual acts, 103, 118-120
Rome, 102
Ruth Simmons, 168

Santa Claus, 78, 159-160
Satish, 76, 159-160
schooling, 12, 21, 24, 43, 100, 109, 126, 129-178
Schwartz & Ogilvy, 157-158, 167
self-consciousness/self-conscious, 22, 25, 38, 55, 65, 75-76, 83
self-revelation, 37
Senge, 65, 149
sexual orientation, 38, 77
Shalvelson & Towne, 3
Shields & Edwards, 64, 69
Shields, 54, 169
Sidorkin, 15, 64, 80-82, 84-88, 151, 171
socioeconomic status, 24, 118, 131, 138, 142, 168
speech/ speech communication 7-9, 32, 35, 39-47, 55, 57-58, 62, 66-68, 83, 95, 109, 111
spiritual/spirituality, 13, 22, 29-30, 153, 157, 159, 163
Starratt, 30
Steinbeck, 83
Swartz, 23

test scores, 49, 86, 123, 172
text, 3, 39, 63, 66-68
time/space continuum, 18, 33, 39, 61, 100
truth, 21, 31, 33, 51, 61, 65-66, 68-69, 77-82, 84-85, 87, 89, 90-94, 96, 104, 151, 153, 158, 170-173, 176-177

Uncle Tom's Cabin, 26
unfinalizeability, 28, 86

utterance, 8-9, 35-36, 41-48, 56, 58-59, 62-63, 67, 110, 127, 158

vitality, 98, 125, 136, 143-145, 161, 165
Voltaire, 18,
Vygotsky, 27

Weber, 144
Wheatley, 167
white flight, 21
word, 41-42

zone of contact, 27-28, 33

Peter Lang
PRIMERS
in Education

Peter Lang Primers are designed to provide a brief and concise introduction or supplement to specific topics in education. Although sophisticated in content, these primers are written in an accessible style making them perfect for undergraduate and graduate classroom use. Each volume includes a glossary of key terms and a References and Resources section.

Other published and forthcoming volumes cover such topics as:

- Standards
- Popular Culture
- Critical Pedagogy
- Literacy
- Higher Education
- John Dewey
- Feminist Theory and Education

- Studying Urban Youth Culture
- Multiculturalism through Postformalism
- Creative Problem Solving
- Teaching the Holocaust
- Piaget and Education
- Deleuze and Education
- Foucault and Education

Look for more Peter Lang Primers to be published soon. To order other volumes, please contact our Customer Service Department:

> 800-770-LANG (within the US)
> 212-647-7706 (outside the US)
> 212-647-7707 (fax)

To find out more about this and other Peter Lang book series, or to browse a full list of education titles, please visit our website:

www.peterlang.com